FAITH
IN THE
FOG

Also by Jeff Lucas

Fiction
Heaven Help Helen Sloane
Up Close and Personal: What Helen Did Next

Nonfiction
Creating a Prodigal-Friendly Church
There Are No Strong People
Seriously Funny (Adrian Plass and Jeff Lucas)
Seriously Funny 2 (Adrian Plass and Jeff Lucas)
Lucas on Life
Will Your Prodigal Come Home?
I Was Just Wandering
Standing on My Knees
Lucas on Life 2
Lucas on Life 3
Lucas Unleashed
Lucas Out Loud
Walking Backwards
Grace Choices
Friends of God (with Cleland Thom)
Gideon: Power from Weakness
Going Public: The Life and Times of Elijah
Rediscovering the Father Heart of God
Life Everyday with Lucas 1
Life Everyday with Lucas 2
Life Everyday with Lucas 3

FAITH

IN THE

FOG

BELIEVING IN WHAT YOU CANNOT SEE

JEFF LUCAS

ZONDERVAN

ZONDERVAN

Faith in the Fog
Copyright © 2013 by Jeff Lucas

This title is also available as a Zondervan ebook. Visit www.zondervan.com/ebooks.

Requests for information should be addressed to:

Zondervan, *Grand Rapids, Michigan* 49530

ISBN 978-0-310-28155-9

International Trade Paper Edition

Cover photography: Tim Hall
Interior design: Katherine Lloyd, The DESK

Printed in the United States of America

14 15 16 17 18 19 /DCI/ 23 22 21 20 19 18 17 16 15 14 13 12 11 10 9 8 7 6 5 4 3 2 1

To Kay,
who has held my hand for years,
but more tightly on foggier days.

• • •

And to all who are learning this truth:
seeing isn't believing.
Then Jesus told him,
"Because you have seen me, you have believed;
blessed are those who have not seen
and yet have believed."
(John 20:29)

CONTENTS

A VERY IMPORTANT FOREWORD

It is, without doubt, my favorite passage of Scripture: the twenty-first chapter of John's gospel.

John wraps up his epic gospel, specifically penned to inspire and nurture faith, with a detailed account of a quiet breakfast shared among friends. The story that unfolds has all the components of an Academy Award–winning story: following deep betrayal, a wounded friendship is repaired by a dramatic reunion and an even deeper reconciliation. There's poetic resonance as the past is recalled. Mystery mingles with clarity, with a prediction of martyrdom, and a confirmation of calling.

A miracle is on the menu as well.

Peter's future hinges on this encounter. And far from being detached from what happened that early morning, John invites us into the episode: there's nourishment and strength for us all now that it's our turn to follow Jesus.

And so, in the pages that follow, I'd like to quietly slip into the little fireside huddle that formed around the fire on that damp, probably foggy morning. I'd be delighted if you'd join me; together we'll eavesdrop on the conversation. Look, there's a vacant spot for us there on those lumpy stones. Our seating arrangements aren't terribly comfortable, but I hope it'll be worth it.

As we settle in, would you do me a kindness?

As someone who talks endlessly about the Bible, I'm convinced that Scripture should be read, allowing it to speak for itself, uncluttered and unspoiled by human comment. And so, for now, let's just read through John's account. That way we'll hear his report firsthand, without any behind-cupped-hand whispers from me.

To make that easier, here it is in both the NIV and *The Message* versions. As a dedicated fan of Eugene Petersen's work, I invite you to read both.

NIV

Afterward Jesus appeared again to his disciples, by the Sea of Galilee. It happened this way: Simon Peter, Thomas (also known as Didymus), Nathanael from Cana in Galilee, the sons of Zebedee, and two other disciples were together. "I'm going out to fish," Simon Peter told them, and they said, "We'll go with you." So they went out and got into the boat, but that night they caught nothing.

Early in the morning, Jesus stood on the shore, but the disciples did not realize that it was Jesus.

He called out to them, "Friends, haven't you any fish?"

"No," they answered.

He said, "Throw your net on the right side of the boat and you will find some." When they did, they were unable to haul the net in because of the large number of fish.

Then the disciple whom Jesus loved said to Peter, "It is the Lord!" As soon as Simon Peter heard him say, "It is the Lord," he wrapped his outer garment around him (for he had taken it off) and jumped into the water. The other disciples followed in the boat, towing the net full of fish, for they were not far from shore, about a hundred yards. When they landed, they saw a fire of burning coals there with fish on it, and some bread.

Jesus said to them, "Bring some of the fish you have just caught."

So Simon Peter climbed back into the boat and dragged the net ashore. It was full of large fish, 153, but even with so many the net was not torn. Jesus said to them, "Come and have breakfast." None of the disciples dared ask him, "Who are you?" They knew it was the Lord. Jesus came, took the bread and gave it to them, and did the same with the fish. This was now the third time Jesus appeared to his disciples after he was raised from the dead.

When they had finished eating, Jesus said to Simon Peter, "Simon son of John, do you love me more than these?"

"Yes, Lord," he said, "you know that I love you."

Jesus said, "Feed my lambs."

Again Jesus said, "Simon son of John, do you love me?"

He answered, "Yes, Lord, you know that I love you."

Jesus said, "Take care of my sheep."

The third time he said to him, "Simon son of John, do you love me?"

Peter was hurt because Jesus asked him the third time, "Do you love me?" He said, "Lord, you know all things; you know that I love you."

Jesus said, "Feed my sheep. Very truly I tell you, when you were younger you dressed yourself and went where you wanted; but when you are old you will stretch out your hands, and someone else will dress you and lead you where you do not want to go." Jesus said this to indicate the kind of death by which Peter would glorify God. Then he said to him, "Follow me!"

Peter turned and saw that the disciple whom Jesus loved was following them. (This was the one who had leaned back against Jesus at the supper and had said, "Lord, who is going to betray you?") When Peter saw him, he asked, "Lord, what about him?"

Jesus answered, "If I want him to remain alive until I return, what is that to you? You must follow me." Because of this, the rumor spread among the believers that this disciple would not die. But Jesus did not say that he would not die; he only said, "If I want him to remain alive until I return, what is that to you?"

THE MESSAGE

After this, Jesus appeared again to the disciples, this time at the Tiberias Sea (the Sea of Galilee). This is how he did it: Simon Peter, Thomas (nicknamed "Twin"), Nathanael from Cana in Galilee, the brothers Zebedee, and two other disciples were together. Simon Peter announced, "I'm going fishing."

The rest of them replied, "We're going with you." They went out and got in the boat. They caught nothing that night. When the sun came up, Jesus was standing on the beach, but they didn't recognize him.

Jesus spoke to them: "Good morning! Did you catch anything for breakfast?"

They answered, "No."

He said, "Throw the net off the right side of the boat and see what happens."

They did what he said. All of a sudden there were so many fish in it, they weren't strong enough to pull it in.

Then the disciple Jesus loved said to Peter, "It's the Master!"

When Simon Peter realized that it was the Master, he threw on some clothes, for he was stripped for work, and dove into the sea. The other disciples came in by boat for they weren't far from land, a hundred yards or so, pulling along the net full of fish. When they got out of the boat, they saw a fire laid, with fish and bread cooking on it.

Jesus said, "Bring some of the fish you've just caught." Simon Peter joined them and pulled the net to shore — 153 big fish! And even with all those fish, the net didn't rip.

Jesus said, "Breakfast is ready." Not one of the disciples dared ask, "Who are you?" They knew it was the Master.

Jesus then took the bread and gave it to them. He did the same with the fish. This was now the third time Jesus had shown himself alive to the disciples since being raised from the dead.

After breakfast, Jesus said to Simon Peter, "Simon, son of John, do you love me more than these?"

"Yes, Master, you know I love you."

Jesus said, "Feed my lambs."

He then asked a second time, "Simon, son of John, do you love me?"

"Yes, Master, you know I love you."

Jesus said, "Shepherd my sheep."

Then he said it a third time: "Simon, son of John, do you love me?"

Peter was upset that he asked for the third time, "Do you love me?" so he answered, "Master, you know everything there is to know. You've got to know that I love you."

Jesus said, "Feed my sheep. I'm telling you the very truth now: When you were young you dressed yourself and went wherever you wished, but when you get old you'll have to stretch out your hands while someone else dresses you and takes you where you don't want to go." He said this to hint at the kind of death by which Peter would glorify God. And then he commanded, "Follow me."

Turning his head, Peter noticed the disciple Jesus loved following right behind. When Peter noticed him, he asked Jesus, "Master, what's going to happen to *him*?"

Jesus said, "If I want him to live until I come again, what's that to you? You—follow me." That is how the rumor got out among the brothers that this disciple wouldn't die. But that is not what Jesus said. He simply said, "If I want him to live until I come again, what's that to you?"

One final thought. *Exegesis* is the word used to describe the detailed investigation and analysis of a biblical text. But when preachers and writers read too much into a text, adding their own presuppositions, agendas, and biases, it's called *eisegesis*.

This book is neither. In the tradition of the rabbis, who would gather around a story and pick away at it, pondering and speculating, considering any number of different interpretations and applications, I'd like to reflect on this breakfast, not insisting that the directions that we take are certain, but rather just allowing this beautiful story to spark our imaginations and hopefully stir our hearts.

I hope that you'll enjoy the result.

Come on.

Let's eat.

PROLOGUE

• • •

ESTRANGED
ON THE SHORE

Why does the sea attract me in the way it does?

E. B. WHITE

Every time we walk along a beach some ancient urge disturbs us so that we find ourselves shedding shoes and garments or scavenging among seaweed and whitened timbers like the homesick refugees of a long war.

LOREN EISELEY

The sea does not reward those who are too anxious, too greedy, or too impatient. One should lie empty, open, choiceless as a beach — waiting for a gift from the sea.

ANNE MORROW LINDBERGH

Anticipation fuels the imagination, and I was desperate to get to that beach.

In my mind's eye, I pictured vast sweeps of sand sloping down to meet the sea, like the endless undulating dunes of the northern Oregon coast, khaki mounds skimmed and renewed every second by wild, sculpting winds. Rocks squatting here and there, inviting clambering, jumping children. Crystal clear pools for them to peer into, darting silver treasures within. Roaming gangs of gulls, angry birds strutting their stuff, heads down, beady-eyed marauders dashing to and fro in their eternal fuss.

Most of all, I wanted to stand very still at the edge of the Sea of Galilee and just breathe in. Surely it would be turquoise in color, gently warm to the toes, the diffused sun rippling the seabed beneath. It would be calm, the rhythm and power of the waves subdued into gentle lapping.

The sea is actually a vast freshwater lake, which is why it's also known as Lake Tiberias. But don't be fooled by this talk of a lake. Without warning, it can be whipped into a furious storm, wild enough to traumatize the most seasoned fisherman. Matthew describes one as being like a watery earthquake. At 680 feet below sea level, the lake is surrounded by ravines and gorges that act like wind tunnels, unleashing unexpected tempests even when the skies above are blue and unthreatening.

But surely there would be no boiling, turbulent waters.

Today, I decided, the beach would be idyllic. A hint of paradise. Serene.

But although the water was millpond calm, the beach was pretty but not stunning. Dull pebbles were strewn over unappealing sand, more muddy brown than gold. And the place was anything but the holy haven of peace I had imagined. Camera-toting tourists scampered around, all smiles and chatter and clicking.

I didn't care. I'd been eager to walk this beach for four decades, and the timing of my pilgrimage was perfect.

The last few days had been bewildering, and I'd promised myself that a trip to the beach would help me find perspective again. Beaches are places of constant renewal, refreshed every few seconds by another surge of water, eradicating footprints, demolishing sandcastles, unsettling and relocating stones. The water doesn't back down from any challenge; even the rocks are ultimately worn down by its insistent ebb and flow. I hoped that its rejuvenating power would help kick-start my sputtering faith.

It was my first trip to Israel, and bewilderment hadn't been part of the plan.

Surely a visit to the land of the Bible would energize my Christianity, I'd thought. I'd discover places that had hitherto just been names on a thin page — familiar names that still seemed distant, that might have been mythical locations in a novel. Made-up places from Christmas plays and children's stories and Sunday morning sermons.

Bethlehem.

Nazareth.

Jerusalem.

To visit the scenery of the big story would surely make it all feel more concrete, more substantial, more true. That's what I had hoped for.

But my trek to Bethlehem had made the familiar nativity story seem vaguer and wholly disconnected from what I saw there. The much-serenaded little town of Bethlehem is a bleak, hopeless place, circled by a wall twice the size of the one that once surrounded East Berlin. Deemed illegal by the International Court of Justice in 2004, the twenty-foot-high wall means that the Palestinians of Bethlehem, Christians and Muslims alike, are a people besieged.

Meeting Christians in Bethlehem, I wept as I heard of their daily struggles, which includes persecution from Muslim extremists in the city. Sixty years ago, 80 percent of the population of Bethlehem was Christians—now it's down to 20 percent. Bethlehem is not a place of peace, of stillness, a place of deep and dreamless sleep, the city the beautiful carol once heralded. Sometimes students at Bethlehem Bible College are harassed by militant Muslims who stand in front of the college building, loudly chanting from the Quran in an attempt to intimidate. Some homes have been firebombed.

But even as these Palestinian followers of Jesus suffer pain that's inflicted by hostility from without, there is another deep wound in their hearts, one that comes from an unexpected source—that of the Christian church, worldwide.

Our brothers and sisters in Bethlehem feel largely ignored by their global Christian family.

Some of us seem to think that to "bless" Israel means that we ignore or even curse Palestinians. This is a strange notion, coupled with the view that supporting Israel means that we endorse everything Israel does in her domestic and foreign policy.

It's an odd view of blessing.

God is the ultimate blesser, and he has never given a blanket endorsement to Israel or indeed any other nation. On the contrary, he sent a whole herd of prophets to confront his forgetful people about their frequent seasons of oppression and injustice.

And so a difficult day spent with those brave Christian leaders in Bethlehem made this sad truth unbearably clear.

Those beleaguered believers feel absolutely alone.

Did you know it would turn out like this, Jesus?

This was the place of beginnings, of stunning good news announced to bleary-eyed shepherds, shivering their way through the graveyard shift. Here angels had lit up the sky and belted out their Savior song. Good news of great joy.

Peace on earth.

Peace on earth?

I certainly didn't see much peace there in that little walled-in town of Bethlehem. And the barrier between the Palestinian believers and their worldwide Christian family seemed as insurmountable as that graffiti-scarred wall.

I ended my day in Bethlehem with a visit to the Church of the Nativity, the basilica built over a cave where the holy family supposedly took shelter. With an obedient star to guide the very first pilgrims, here a virgin gave birth, wise men presented extravagant gifts, and those anxious shepherds worshiped. But despite it being the oldest continually used church building in the world, the church is in a dangerous state of disrepair. The roof timbers have not been replaced since the nineteenth century and are now rotting. Rainwater constantly seeps into the building, damaging the ancient mosaics and paintings, and creating a constant risk of an electrical fire. The three custodians of the building—the Greek and Armenian Ortho-dox Churches, together with a Franciscan order—would need to cooperate to enable the restoration of these works. But cooperation has not happened for hundreds of years.

This place, this Bethlehem, was chosen for the arrival of the One whose name is Wonderful. But instead of experiencing a rush of wonder, I wrestled with niggling anxiety. As each visitor filed down into the little grotto that houses the site where baby Jesus first saw the light of day, and took their turn to kneel on the marble floor and kiss the silver star that marks the spot, I worried. An avalanche of questions rolled over my mind.

Is all this floor-kissing superstitious tokenism rather than worship?

Even if this really is the precise location of the birth of Jesus, does it matter? Surely it's the significance of his birth that matters, not revering the supposed place where it happened?

What does God think about these shrines?

And a practical question, one concerning public health.

Surely all that reverent kissing means that silver star is coated in spit? That's a toxic health hazard.

At last it was my turn to pick my way down the shadowy steps to the holy spot. The air was heavy with the smell of candle wax and incense.

The incense stuck in my throat. I tried to cough reverently.

I knelt and wondered what to do.

So perhaps he was here, all those years ago. Should I proffer a kiss? Instead, the persistent question circled my brain again, like a pesky mosquito that resists swatting: Did you know it would turn out like this, Jesus?

Guilt washed over me. Right there, where it allegedly had all started, I was wrestling with that question rather than offering heartfelt worship.

I stayed for a few seconds, desperate to frame a concise thought, offer a substantial sentence of gratitude. But I knew my time was short. The next pilgrims waited in line, eager for their big moment with the silver star. I hurried out, my head cluttered.

Now, two days later, I was bone weary of the hubbub of Jerusalem, with its frantic markets and gaggles of devout boys and men sweating in tall black hats, ringlets dangling, heads bobbing at the Western Wall, strutting their stuff, even as the amplified call to Muslim prayer droned from the Temple Mount. I was tired by another day of Christian excursions and spiritual tourism, and I didn't want to hear one more time that St. Someone of Somewhere had sipped a cappuccino in this very place thousands of years ago.

But I thought I'd try again. Despite the gloom of Bethlehem, I was still hoping for an epiphany at the epicenter of it all for Christian pilgrims, the Church of the Holy Sepulcher, the church built on the traditional site of Christ's crucifixion, burial, and resurrection.

There, at Gospel Ground Zero, I anticipated encounter.

But the despair I felt was suffocating as I wandered around the candlelit sepulcher. The debacle of the Church of the Nativity in Bethlehem was being played out there too. Each section of the building is guarded—literally—by priests from the Armenian, Roman Catholic, and Greek, Eastern, Coptic, Syrian, and Ethiopian Orthodox churches, all of whom are jealous to protect "their" territory to the point of violence.

On a hot summer day in 2002, a Coptic monk shifted his chair from its agreed spot into the shade, which was interpreted as a hostile move by the Ethiopians. Eleven were hospitalized after the resulting fracas. A fistfight in 2004 broke out when someone left a chapel door open, giving the impression of disrespect. Righteous indignation led to some unholy punching. Then, in 2008, police were called to a near riot, and later the same year, another fight broke out between Armenian and Greek monks.

There is a balcony above the church's entrance. A ladder sits there, leaned against the wall where it has been since 1839, when it appeared in a painting from that year. No one dares move that ladder, because it is parked in a common area, and to relocate it would be interpreted as staking a claim for that balcony. That ladder is a symbol of fighting.

Pettiness.

Territorialism.

That church marks the place where the old wooden cross is supposed to have stood.

The cross.

Because of what happened at that cross, peace with God is offered. Peace with each other is possible. But wandering around the church, all I could think about was another wooden monument.

The ladder.

I wandered into one of the side chapels where a monk was fussing at the altar with the heavy gilt candlesticks that squatted on white cloth. His errand finished, he gathered his stuff and turned to go. I caught his eye and offered a warm smile. But his face was fixed, his eyes cold.

I didn't exist.

Just another tourist.

He bustled out, set on fulfilling his religious duties.

As I hurried away from the sepulcher, I fought to subdue an overwhelming desire to just walk away from Christianity, to turn my back on it all, once and for all, to shrug it off as a good dream gone terribly bad.

Did you know it would turn out like this, Jesus?

I'd hoped for an epiphany. Joy. Confirmation. Instead, I was in a fog. I had hoped for clarity, but instead I was lost in the mist, unable to see even a few yards ahead of me. Where might all this confusion lead?

My heart heavy, I checked out of my hotel and headed north for Galilee.

There I would find the place where bread was multiplied to feed five thousand.

I'd visit Capernaum, where Peter lived with his extended family, and where Jesus preached his first, one-sentence sermon.

But I also had another destination in mind, just a couple of miles from Capernaum.

Tabgha.

The beach.

• • •

Located on the northwest shore of the Sea of Galilee, Tabgha is the supposed location where Jesus, after his resurrection, appeared a third time to the disciples as a stranger on the shore.

For Peter, this was the beach where everything changed. Here, an exhausted, confused fisherman embraced a to-the-death martyr's calling.

On this beach, his shame was washed away, like a signature in the sand eradicated by a surge of bubbling surf.

His purpose was reaffirmed.

His bewilderment was banished, his focus regained.

A few weeks after their meeting on this beach, the disciples would experience another epic event: the Day of Pentecost. They were fueled by the power of the Holy Spirit even as they huddled nervously in prayer.

On that Pentecost day, Peter would step up to the plate, plant his feet, and begin his role as a bold spokesman for the infant church. Head- and heart-turning miracles would pulse from his shadow. The coward would become a hero, later enduring insults, threats, prison, beatings, and ultimately execution.

But how might history have been different if Peter had never even made it to the upper room, excluded by his own failures, disqualifying himself because he'd made such a mess of things?

Judas had betrayed Jesus for cash. Unable to live with the shame of that, he'd chosen suicide, oblivion at the end of a rope.

While Peter didn't actually sell his friend out to the authorities, he did betray Jesus to save his own skin. What might have happened to Peter if he had not been able to receive the grace that forgave his treacherous words? The beachside breakfast was a major turning point for Peter—it was his pathway to the Day of Pentecost and beyond.

And so I decided to get to Tabgha by boat, a brief voyage across the Sea of Galilee.

I knew the beach would not be unsullied by the religious fervor that rushes to build shrines. This would be yet another "holy" site.

Sure enough, the beach has a church building to mark the spot, the Church of the Primacy of St. Peter. Although the current building is only eighty years old, there has been a shrine-church here since the fourth century. It's built around a rock, and tradition says that it was here that Jesus served that historic breakfast to Peter and his friends.

The boat trip was exhilarating and amusing. Glad to be in the fresh air and rustic beauty of the Sea of Galilee, I was starting to feel alive again. Here Jesus spent much of his life, and it was easier to imagine him enjoying glorious sunsets and misty mornings. The shrines of Jerusalem and Bethlehem had distanced me from him, and had even made his mission seem somewhat farcical: he had not died to create a church ridden with mindless tradition, where clerics fight over ladders. But he had traversed this sea, ridden out its storms, even walked on its surface.

Even the antics of the boat captain couldn't dampen my enthusiasm for the beach. After asking what my religion was and what denomination I was from, he selected a music CD from a large collection: organs and choirs for Anglicans, drums and guitars for Pentecostals and charismatics, and a sung mass for Catholics. I smiled as we floated across the beautiful lake, accompanied by the strangely incongruous soft-rock anthems from Hillsong Australia.

The captain was a good host. He was obviously familiar with the story of Peter and his friends hauling a miraculous catch of fish out of these waters, as the mysterious man on shore told them where to cast their net. A hundred yards from the beach, the captain produced a net of his own and asked me if I'd like to try my hand at Peter's craft.

Just as Peter had done at Jesus' command, I cast the net on the right-hand side of the boat. To do anything else would have seemed wrong, faintly rebellious, as if I knew better. It still came up empty.

The captain tapped his CD player into silence mid-song and docked the boat.

My moment had arrived. We made our way around to the front gate, the entryway to the church and the beach. Suddenly my heart sank as I approached the gate.

It was guarded by a scowling priest, surveying every visitor like an ecclesiastical sentry. I thought back to the grim-faced monks and priests at the sepulcher. But I dismissed the image, and with the sun on my back, I smiled at the priest as I passed him by. By now I was excited. I didn't want to go inside the church; instead I just headed past it, straight to that shoreline.

But I almost didn't make it.

As I went to walk by the poker-faced priest, he jumped up and snapped something at me in Hebrew.

"S'leecha!"

I'm not sure why I momentarily searched my memory banks for a translation.

My Hebrew is limited to one word. Shalom. And that didn't seem to be what he was saying.

I started to walk on, but he yelled and pointed directly at me, speaking in heavily accented English.

"Hey! You! You can't go in. It's a holy place. You're not allowed."

A lot can happen inside my head in a second or two. For an illogical moment, I thought that somehow this stern cleric knew my deepest flaws, my darkest moments of shame. Ridiculous though it sounds, I wondered if perhaps he just knew that utterly holy I was not, and so was blocking my way to the beach. In a world of ultra high-speed everything, some of us can hurtle into irrational guilt and shame in a millisecond. Seeing the look of shock on my face, the priest used his pointing finger to jab at a sign, one that I had not noticed before. In four languages — Hebrew, German, French, and English — a two sentence prohibition was clear:

No shorts.

There was even a drawing of a pair of shorts in a circle, with a line drawn through them, like a no-smoking sign.

Yikes. This was bad news indeed.

I was wearing shorts.

I felt the pitying eyes of others behind me, waiting in line. Some glared at the blasphemer that was apparently me, a good candidate for a stoning.

I wanted to protest. The blistering heat meant that shorts were the only sensible attire—unless, of course, you plan on visiting a holy site.

And I had planned to do just that. I'd come too far to miss the beach. And so, pride cast aside, I decided to beg. When all else fails, plead.

The folds of the old priest's face seemed to fall most naturally into a frown; a scowl had been his facial expression of choice for some time. He stood up, hands on hips, a look of disdain locked in place, his posture screaming the message: I'm in absolute charge here, and don't you forget it.

I stammered out an apology.

Explained that this was the last day of the trip, my final opportunity to visit the beach.

Promised that I wouldn't try to go into the church and defile it by my startlingly white legs.

I could tell he was in a quandary. He wanted to let me in, and he wanted to maintain his authority. He had to compromise, but his suggestion was alarming.

"Pull your shorts down and cover as much of your legs as possible. Then you can go in."

It's not a pleasant picture, is it? Rather obviously, if you yank your shorts down a couple of inches, you maintain your modesty at the front, but your back is ... exposed.

Okay, I'm trying to be discreet. It's your backside that's in view.

And so that's how I finally made it to the beach. I walked there awkwardly, because my shorts were too far down my legs. I stood on the beach, feeling ridiculous and exposed, wondering if those camera-festooned tourists were confused as to why anyone would visit this place while revealing the crack of his rear end.

On the bland sand at last, I kicked at a pebble angrily, smothered by shame because I wasn't wearing the right uniform, stung by being made to feel like an outsider. I had felt like a refugee at Bethlehem, unable to wholeheartedly join in with all that kneeling and self-crossing and kissing. The sepulcher, with its shadowy territories and its immovable ladder, far from inspiring my faith, made me feel like I wanted to run away from faith at high speed. I felt overwhelmed by all I perceived that was wrong—a feeling that had become all too familiar to me.

Sometimes I feel like an outsider in church. I feel that when a hollow cliché is palmed off as a profound truth. I feel it when an evangelist declares that a wheelchair-bound man is healed, but even as the crowd cheers, I see him wince in familiar pain. When fellow leaders act so anointed, so very certain of themselves, I feel like I'm on the outside. I feel like an outsider when Christians snarl and bite, and when heaven seems silent and has been for a while.

And sometimes I'm overwhelmed by all that is wrong with me. When all of my resolution is as dust and I am flushed with the shame of failure, I feel like an outsider.

Having finally made it to the beach, instead of experiencing a warm glow as a pilgrim, I was red faced with embarrassment. It wasn't just about me, hapless in my impossibly stretched shorts. While I stood at the gate and frantically tried to stretch them down over my knees, I watched as a bright, smiling young couple were turned away from the gate because she too was wearing shorts. Their smiles were quickly wiped off their faces. I wondered if they thought that God was similar to the glowering priest guarding the beach: tetchy, illogical, unwelcoming.

The God who rages at those who wear shorts.

Did you know it would turn out like this, Jesus?

And then it dawned on me that this beach was just the place for me. Peter came here when he felt he would probably be rejected, when he felt like a stranger to grace, when he felt like he didn't fit in and probably never would. The beach welcomes awkward, stumbling, faintly ridiculous outsiders like me. And, if you're happy to line up with such an odd crowd—one like you.

• • •

The beach at Tabgha is often shrouded with fog, especially in the early morning hours. Seeing anything much is difficult on those days.

This is a book about living with faith in the fog. Although I will share some of my own experience with depression, this book is not just about depression: others with expertise far beyond mine have written about that. Rather, I want us to walk in Peter's sandals for a while and ponder what it means to call ourselves Christian when life is tough, tragic, hard, and just plain boring.

I'd like us to ask some hard questions as we sit on the beach together:

How do you keep believing in what you cannot see?
Why are so many Christians shame addicts when the gospel is supposed to be such good news of forgiveness and liberation?
Why do we keep coming up with the same old clichés and slogans, which we dump on those who are suffering?
How can we prevent ourselves from becoming territorial, petty people?
Have we painted an inaccurate portrait of what it means to be a follower of Christ, which quickly leads many to disappointment when they find out that the life of faith is not the breathless adventure that was advertised?
Do the eyes of faith give us the 20/20 vision that we sometimes claim?

I'd like to intertwine reflections on Peter's beach experience with some snapshots from my own journey. I'm embarrassed that some might feel that parallels between my story and Peter's are inappropriate or even pretentious. But be assured by my conviction that my affinity with him is simply as a fellow failure, nothing more. Perhaps you feel similarly at home with the headstrong fisherman, aware as you are of your own flaws and failures.

Peter makes good company. Ask any congregation to vote for their favorite Bible character apart from Jesus, and Peter usually wins by a landslide. His fragility is strangely comforting. So let's listen in on the conversation between Jesus and his friends, especially Peter. And as we do, perhaps we'll be nudged to have some conversations with Jesus ourselves. He listened well that day. He still does.

1

...

TIME TRAPPED

Afterward Jesus appeared again to his disciples, by the Sea of Galilee. It happened this way: Simon Peter, Thomas (also known as Didymus), Nathanael from Cana in Galilee, the sons of Zebedee, and two other disciples were together. "I'm going out to fish," Simon Peter told them, and they said, "We'll go with you."

JOHN 21:1 – 3

Nostalgia is the suffering caused by an unappeased yearning to return.

MILAN KUNDERA

No man ever stepped into the same river twice, because it's not the same river, and it's not the same man.

HERACLITUS

There are moments when I feel "time trapped," hemmed in by the present, and wish I could break free from the shackles of what is and go back to what was.

Recently, after enjoying a blissful holiday with our closest friends, we stayed on at the hotel for a few extra days after they had left. But although the sun still shone, some emotional clouds rolled in. The familiar landscape we had enjoyed together, the coffee shops and poolside chairs, all lost their allure because our friends were gone; our joy was overshadowed by nostalgia—or perhaps something deeper.

Sometimes the feeling goes beyond sentimentality or the natural sadness that comes when a happy season ends. I have awakened in the middle of the night feeling breathless, on the verge of a panic attack, because of the unbridgeable chasm between my present and my past. It's brutal to face the fact that everything, however beautiful, is temporary.

But we all have to face this harsh truth.

Birth jettisons us into endless travel, and absolutely no stopping is allowed. However good the day, life insists that we move onward, always. We are pinioned by time, which does not only march on, but demands that we keep in strict step with it.

And as I rue the truth that what was will never be again, I'm not alone. Theologian and writer Monica Coleman says:

I've never thought of myself as someone who clings to the past ... I want to go back in time. When I put it that way, I know it's not possible. I know I cannot do anything over. I know I cannot be who I was ... in the space amidst the knowledge that I can't go back in time, my inability to see in front of myself, and my desperate need for peace, I need the past. I need the good parts of the past.... I need to remember that I have been happy before. I need to remember the faith that I can't feel at the moment. I need the past to come to me.

The clock ticks, always forward, never back. The second hand sweeps slowly around. Perhaps that's one reason why the gaggle of weary fishermen headed for the familiar territory of Galilee. It wasn't just because it was home.

Perhaps they needed the past to come to them once more.

• • •

Some grim-faced writers and commentators rush to condemn the disciples as they trekked back to Galilee. The fishers of men should never have gone back to fishing for fish, they mutter. That little fishing trip has been described by commentators as "apostasy," "unthinkable behavior," and as "aimless activity undertaken in desperation."

Bah! Humbug. Tough words — and unjustified, I think.

Surely the criticism is ill-founded, not least because an angelic messenger promised the disciples they would meet Jesus in Galilee. Jesus himself had reiterated the command to gather in Galilee when he appeared to the worshiping women on Easter morning. They weren't actually told to take to the water, but surely there was a more mundane reason for that fishing trip.

The disciples still had to eat.

If some commentators line up to rebuke the fishermen, there's no stiff rebuke from Jesus when he arrived at the beach. Arriving there when the hapless gaggle were probably ready to abandon their futile fishing trip, he even helped them with their net-casting technique. In fact, when Peter realizes it's Jesus giving the instructions, he jumps out of the boat and heads toward shore — hardly the behavior of a fugitive caught in the act of doing something suspect.

How swiftly we can condemn what Jesus welcomes and blesses.

Rather than question their motives for the fishing trip, we'd do better to consider the disciples' mood that morning, for if we are to grasp the significance of what happened on the beach, a sense of their emotional condition that day is important.

The resurrected Jesus arrived and did some cooking, not just because this was an appointment set on his kingdom timetable, but because his somewhat exhausted and confused friends really needed that meal, the silence shared during the cooking of it, and the conversation that followed.

Did the disciples feel the hollow ache of "time trap" as they trudged back to Galilee from Jerusalem? At last they were home again, a welcome sight after the cataclysmic events of the first Easter in Jerusalem.

But they were home alone without Jesus.

The familiar sights, sounds, and smells of the Galilee would have constantly reminded them of headier days gone by, days that now seemed gone forever.

We look at the cross and the resurrection through the lens of the New Testament, with the clarity that two thousand years of theological reflection brings to that universe-changing weekend. But they did not have that same lens.

He had been very dead. Now he was very much alive. Their reaction was not just one of exhilaration or understanding—they were riding on an emotional and theological roller coaster.

They had begun to mourn his awful death, but now their minds and hearts were assaulted by the truth that their friend and rabbi was alive once more. Even walking through the extremities of those three days could have caused some of them to totter into emotional breakdown. The little band of friends and followers were confused, believing, and doubting—all at once.

Consider some of the phrases used to describe their emotional

condition after the resurrection, emotions caused by the news that
Jesus was risen, and by his later appearing among them:

> They were startled. Frightened. They thought they'd seen a
>   ghost.
> They were troubled. Doubting. Joy mingled with their
>   amazement.
> They needed to have their minds "opened" to understand.
> They were afraid yet filled with joy.
> They worshiped, but some doubted.
> They were trembling, bewildered, and afraid.
> They did not believe. They stubbornly refused to believe.
> They gathered fearfully behind locked doors.
> They were overjoyed.

There were a myriad of questions:

> What does this mean?
> What's next?
> What will become of us?
> What are we supposed to do?

And most importantly this, from those who had lived for three
years with him:

How can we live now—without Jesus?

His friends had to grieve this reality: he was alive again, but he
would never be with them in the same way that he had been, every
day, face-to-face, for those three amazing years. Bible scholar Don
Carson sums up their mood: "There is neither the joy nor the assurance, not to mention the sense of mission and the spirit of unity, that
characterized the church when freshly endowed with the promised
Spirit."

We often overlook that Jesus took the disciples through what must have been an unforgettable forty-day training period between his resurrection and ascension. We're not told much about what happened in those six weeks except that he appeared to them and spoke about the kingdom of God.

But this much was still true: he was going away, and they would have to live with the pain of that, even though he'd tried to prepare them for the parting.

And so a Galilean homecoming for the disciples was surely bittersweet. Poignant memories were stirred by places where they'd been with him, so many familiar trails walked and hillsides climbed.

Together.

It was here that the remarkable journey had begun, as Jesus chose Galilee as the venue to launch his ministry.

Here the disciples had first bumped into him and responded to his incredible invitation that changed absolutely everything for them: he had offered to become their rabbi. Most likely they had no idea what "fishing for men" meant, nor any notion about the epic nature of their mission, but the strange compulsion to be with him overruled their many unanswered questions, at least for a while.

Jesus began his preaching ministry at the little synagogue in Capernaum, a shoreline village. Later he would tour the synagogues of Galilee, primarily focusing on deliverance, which certainly turned many heads, catapulting him into a celebrity spotlight, a role he always resisted.

What a strange teacher he had been, so revolutionary and yet apparently shy of the huge numbers that sought him out. But still they came, grabbing, clamoring for him. Some were so frantic they even vandalized a roof, hacking through it to lower their disabled friend to Jesus.

At times, things must have seemed to the disciples that things were getting out of hand: the security concern as the ebbing crowds pressed closer, causing them to hastily push a boat offshore, turning it into a makeshift pulpit; the catering crisis—saved by a packed lunch and a miracle—five thousand fed to the full with leftovers that filled baskets. The disciples had watched wide-eyed as lepers were made clean, not only physically healed, but released from the exile that leprosy had sentenced them to. Now they were welcomed in from the cold, taking their places in the community once more. And then there was that life-threatening storm on the unpredictable Sea of Galilee. They had watched, terrified, as Jesus strode across the foamy tips of the boiling waves. Even the gale-force winds had calmed at his word.

Here in Galilee, beggars' banquets were thrown for ladies of the night and other "undesirables." Crooked tax collectors joined in the feasts and promptly offered extravagant refunds.

Here too there was scandal and outrage. Religious barons were mortified at his teaching and outraged by his eating and drinking habits. The occupying Romans were also a constant worry. Galilee had been a breeding ground for political revolutionaries, and so the Romans had brutally stomped on any would-be Messiah figures, determined to stifle any emerging resistance movements. No wonder Jesus insisted that people who experienced his healing power keep quiet about it—he and his team didn't need any unwelcome attention from the authorities.

But Galilee's scenery reminded them of more than those tense, powerful, adventurous, jaw-dropping episodes. There were memories that triggered tears as well, recollections that stung them with regret.

The winds and the waves had obeyed him, but the disciples—and some who were more on the fringes of his group—hadn't always been so compliant. There was the dark season when many decided that they no longer wanted to be with Jesus. Watching the backs of those who walked away sliced him to the heart, and he asked them: Will you leave also?

They'd promised faithfulness. But eventually, of course, they'd do exactly that.

Leave.

He was arrested, and everyone fled.

And there was the unbearably painful day when his mother and brothers traveled to Galilee to stage an intervention. They'd planned to take him home forcibly, fearing he'd lost his mind.

And had they, the disciples, lost their minds when here, in Galilee, they'd argued about who was the greatest among them? What were they thinking?

In Galilee, the happiest and saddest memories mingled for these friends and apprentices of Jesus. But surely one among them felt the greatest impact of all that had happened there.

Peter.

• • •

They'd already met privately once. There had been a previous meeting one-on-one between the resurrected Jesus and Peter. It's mentioned twice in Scripture but was obviously highly confidential, because absolutely nothing is known about it, apart from the timing: Easter Day. Of all of the conversations that have ever taken place in history, perhaps that's the one I'd most like to eavesdrop on.

Imagine it. Friend turned betrayer meets the one he betrayed.

How did the conversation begin?

What was Jesus' tone of voice, his facial expression?

Did Peter cry? Was his denial even mentioned?

As we'll see, the breakfast discussion between Jesus and Peter hints that perhaps it was not raised during their first meeting, which says something very intriguing about Jesus.

We'll never know for sure, but regardless, consider this: that first face-to-face meeting that Peter had with the resurrected Jesus didn't resolve everything.

Some Christians are addicted to the instant. They insist that if we could all just have epic encounters with God — or better still, revival — then we and our culture would quickly get "fixed." I admire their tenacity. But the suggestion that growth and development comes from attending more electrifying meetings or revival services can create false expectations and immaturity. Even though Peter had already experienced a personal, private consultation with the risen Christ, that didn't resolve all of his "issues." That would still take a lifetime. Discipleship is not just about us craving big moments and major encounters; it involves our slow, sometimes painful growth in the day-in, day-out experiences in the academy called life.

That said, those moments when God meets us can be a vital part of our ongoing journey — and Jesus had another one of those planned for Peter and his friends.

But as we'll see, sometimes God meets us in ways that we least expect.

• • •

Was there anything, apart from hunger, that prompted Peter to plan a fishing trip that day?

Perhaps so, because it was here, on the Sea of Galilee, that the most exhilarating experience of his life took place. He'd done the impossible — he'd walked on water. Never mind that after a few steps he sank. The fact is, he had felt the unearthly sensation of water becoming solid underfoot as he briefly strode across the waves.

Or did it feel like that at all? Did he hover across the top of the water, his feet skimming the turbulent surface, his legs and thighs soaked by the icy spray?

Even more amazing was that the walk across the waves had been Peter's idea. He'd suggested it to Jesus, who had agreed. What had being around Jesus done to him, that he could have come up with such a fantastic proposal?

As he decided to put the family boat back in the water, did he shake his head and wonder if it had all just been a dream? Perhaps other snapshots from the last three years were racing through his mind.

When he'd first met Jesus, introduced by his brother Andrew, he would have been clueless about the roller-coaster ride ahead. All he knew was that there was something about this man that both repelled and attracted him, a confusing entwining of emotions.

On one hand, there was something about Jesus—they way he looked, the way he spoke—that made Peter feel undone, incomplete, and sinful. This was more than just masculine competitiveness and intimidation. At their first meeting, Peter had felt so overwhelmed by shame that he'd even asked this fascinating stranger to go away. Helpfully, Jesus hadn't complied and instead offered some kind assurance: Don't be afraid. You'll be a fisher of men.

Perhaps that's why he'd felt such a powerful compulsion to be with Jesus. He was so disturbing and yet so reassuring. Jesus had interrupted and altered the life of Peter, a man with a small business and domestic responsibilities (he had a wife—that's how he got a mother-in-law) and who lived in an extended-family home. Yet Peter chose to abandon caution and follow this most unusual man. Perhaps we've done the same, offering our lives to what at times seems so certain and then, sometimes, so tenuous and even implausible, yet still we follow.

Jesus can prove difficult to live with, and yet we can't live without him.

And so Peter had followed, with immediate, startling results.

It was in his own home in Capernaum that Peter first saw a power unleashed that was unlike anything he'd ever witnessed. His mother-in-law had been struck down by a severe fever, but she'd recovered at a touch from Jesus. One moment she was bedridden, the next she was fixing them a meal. And that's when everything quickly became even more bewildering.

Later that same night, like a scene from hell, hordes of demon-tormented and sick people began showing up at Peter's house. And as the fisherman watched, evil spirits and devastating diseases were sent packing at Jesus' word.

Cataclysmic events birth multitudes of questions, and through-out his friendship with Jesus, Peter had never been short of ques-tions or reluctant to ask them. Willing to speak up when others were silent, ready to blurt out what others only dared to think, he was ideally situated to inquire, privileged as he was to be part of the inner cabinet around Jesus that was James, John, and himself. Those three had front-row viewing of some episodes that the other nine disciples were excluded from.

Like the day they arrived at the home of a young girl who had just died. Jesus ejected the wailing, garment-tearing professional mourners, and only Peter, James, John, and the girl's stunned parents witnessed her being raised.

Then there was the transfiguration experience on the mountain-side that only the triumvirate were privy to. It would have been a long climb to the summit; thinner air and an arduous day's hiking had taken its toll.

They were sleepy.

But the trio had no idea that this was an epic, red-letter day, nothing less than one of the most momentous episodes in human history. They caught a glimpse of Christ's true glory, as he was trans-figured — metamorphosed — before their eyes. Just as Moses had glimpsed the glory of God on a mountain, so now Peter and his two friends saw who Jesus really was and is.

Their unique privilege meant unique intimacy with Jesus as he summoned the three to share his deepest pain, drawing them into a little huddle in Gethsemane.

The other nine disciples heard Jesus speak tens of thousands of words, but in that garden of twisted, tortured trees, he shared the secrets of his heart with only his closest confidantes. And so naturally Peter felt able to ask those questions of his.

And how he asked.

He'd questioned the meaning of Jesus' parables, which was good, because that was the point.

He asked about forgiveness. How many times is enough?

Peter took on some of the tasks and put forward some of the questions that the others felt awkward with. When Jesus slipped away for some peace and quiet and prayer, it was Peter who had hunted him down.

Hey. Don't you know everyone's looking for you?

Together with James, John, and Andrew, Peter had privately quizzed Jesus about end-time theology. And Peter did more than ask questions. He was bold and often told Jesus exactly what was on his mind, unafraid to say that he and the other disciples had paid a high price to join the team. But despite all those days spent together ambling down dusty roads, the questions, the teaching, the stunning signs and wonders, Jesus was still an enigma to Peter.

For starters, he was unpredictable in his methods. He went to the home of that dead girl, Jairus' daughter, and raised her up. But when a Roman centurion approached him, begging for healing for a member of his household, he didn't bother to go to the house. He just spoke the word.

Done.

He'd put his fingers into people's ears, and slapped globs of spit mixed with mud onto blind eyes. He'd draw a crowd and then apparently run from it, break off an important conference with religious leaders to chatter with and bless some children.

Sometimes it all got so frustrating that Peter and his friends tried to intervene, to manage Jesus. That's never going to work.

They tried to send those parents away, who were desperate for Jesus to put a hand of blessing upon their children. That didn't go well. And looking back, it seemed absurd because Jesus had clearly told them to welcome children in his name.

Then there was that "best of times, worst of times" episode that Peter must have recalled with a cringe.

Peter had affirmed his belief that Jesus was the Messiah, a groundbreaking insight that Jesus celebrated as coming from heaven. But then, the very next second, Peter ruined it all. Right on the heels of revelation came a huge blunder, and a very serious one at that, as Peter, concerned for Jesus' safety, took Jesus aside, rebuked him, and tried to choreograph what should happen next.

That didn't go well either.

Suddenly Jesus turned around and put Peter in his place with words that were witheringly blunt: "Get behind me, Satan! You do not have in mind the concerns of God, but merely human concerns."

It hadn't been the first time that Peter's mouth had gotten him into trouble. Quite literally, the word of the Lord came to him, saying ... be quiet.

Overwhelmed by the terrifying experience of the transfiguration, Peter tried to be helpful but was completely impractical. Hoping to make this amazing encounter last and lasting, he babbled on about his plan to build shelters for Jesus, Moses, and Elijah. He didn't know what he was saying. Perhaps Peter was not just guilty of verbal diarrhea, but actually completely misunderstood that this glory was only temporary. A cross loomed large on the horizon, and Peter desperately wanted Jesus to avoid it. Now that glory shone all around, with even Moses and Elijah arriving on the scene, perhaps the agony ahead could be prevented. Peter is surely like us all: glory sounds wonderful, unless the pathway to it is paved with pain. We'd prefer to take a shortcut, please.

And divine encounter usually spawns more questions than answers. No wonder Peter wanted to stay for a while; it was another opportunity to have his ten thousand questions answered.

How did it feel when fire came down on that soaked sacrifice on Mount Carmel, Elijah?

Moses, why did you get angry that day and strike the rock? Was it fair that you were denied the Promised Land?

But then a cloud descended and a voice spoke.

Listen.

There were, of course, other failures.

In Gethsemane, in Jesus' hour of dire need, when there was something that they could have actually done for him, they'd fallen asleep—not once, but three times. They felt so ashamed that they were speechless.

They'd been so slow to learn. Jesus had spoken plainly about dying and being raised again. Toward the end, he laid it all out— but they hadn't grasped it. And in the end, they'd all run for their lives, but not before Peter's bungled attempt to defend Jesus with a sword had gone disastrously wrong: a young man temporarily lost his ear in the fracas, until Jesus called a halt to the fight and healed the man.

And so, for whatever reason, and despite his insistence that he'd be faithful to the end, even if everyone else let Jesus down, Peter crumbled.

He denied even knowing Jesus.

Backed it up with some colorful curses.

Underscored it no less than three times.

And then, there had been the look. That look. Bloodied by the Roman pummeling, spindles of spit drooping from his beard, Jesus had turned and just looked straight at Peter. Just then the rooster crowed for the third time.

No words. None were needed.

Then the tears came. Bitter tears, soul-wrenching sobs that racked his body.

There was no time for apologies.

A show trial.

Crucifixion.

Despair.

Fear.

Bewildering news.

The tomb is empty. Angels have been sighted. And then Jesus himself is there, right with them. He was dead, bloodied, broken. Now he is alive.

Jesus appears to Peter one on one — and then he appears to Peter and the other ten. Thomas misses it. He continues to live up to his name and carries on doubting.

There's a week, a very long week, and then Jesus appears again, and this time Thomas is there. He believes.

But since then ... nothing.

Passionate, questioning, committed, frail Peter, so desperate to please, is so bewildered and disoriented by all that has happened. During the last three years, he'd experienced bone-deep weariness, heart-stopping terror, and laugh-out-loud exhilaration. There was deep, shoulder-shaking belly laughter one moment and floods of tears the next. But he knew this: he had never felt so utterly alive.

Would he ever be fully alive again?

It was time to head for the beach, to find something substantial he could easily do without having to tax his overwrought brain.

Of course, he'd go fishing. That would clear his head. The rhythmic lapping of waves on the side of the boat would be therapeutic. A hearty meal would follow. Announcing his little voyage to the others, they decided to join him.

That's not surprising, because it's clear from the Greek text that Peter's choice of words served as an invitation. This was, "Who's up for some fishing?" rather than "I want to be alone."

Togetherness is an antidote for confusion.

And so the little band headed for the boat.

Thomas, nicknamed "the twin," the famous unless-I-see-it-I-won't-believe-it doubter, had catapulted from cynic to worshiper in one epic meeting with Jesus, declaring, "My Lord and my God."

Nathaniel, famous for his low opinion of Jesus' home of Nazareth, was convinced that nothing good could come out of that hick town. But all that changed when Philip told him about Jesus; they met, and Nathaniel was stunned as Jesus declared him to be a man of integrity. But his mouth dropped open wider when Jesus described how he'd "seen" Nathaniel standing under a fig tree, stunning evidence of supernatural revelation. Quickly, Nathaniel had declared that Jesus was the Son of God, the Messiah.

James and John went along too. Sons of Zebedee by birth, "sons of thunder" by temperament, they were seasoned fishermen in business with their father.

And two others, unnamed.

As Peter clambered into the boat, he surely felt warm anticipation about their outing.

At least this was something that he knew he could do well. He'd lost his own self-respect, he'd lost the opportunity to be faithful, he'd lost so much.

Fishing — he still had that left. His profession. This he could do.

At least, that's what he hoped.

2

• • •

A BROKEN PIER

Illusions commend themselves to us because they save us pain and allow us to enjoy pleasure instead. We must therefore accept it without complaint when they sometimes collide with a bit of reality against which they are dashed to pieces.

SIGMUND FREUD

I started writing about my own experiences to rid myself of the shame that came from hiding my depressions from most of the people around me. I also wanted to show how a minister and theologian struggles with faith in the midst of living with a depressive condition: I yell at God; I believe some scriptures are lies; I grow impatient; I find holiness in new places; I create rituals; I lean on God.

MONICA A. COLEMAN

Now faith, in the sense in which I am here using the word, is the art of holding on to things your reason has once accepted, in spite of your changing moods. For moods will change, whatever view your reason takes.

C. S. LEWIS

About midnight the fog shut down again denser than before. One could almost "stand on it." It continued so for a number of days, the wind increasing to a gale. The waves rose high, but I had a good ship. Still, in the dismal fog I felt myself drifting into loneliness, an insect on the straw in the midst of the elements.

CAPT. JOSHUA SLOCUM

t is another rather plain beach. Even the name of the place is jarring:

Bognor.

Anything with the word *bog* in it sounds rather unattractive. And this is a town that heavily relies on tourism.

A classic British seaside resort, all cotton candy and tacky T-shirts, it's actually called Bognor Regis, because King George V chose to convalesce there in 1929. The extended royal visit prompted the town council to approach the king's private secretary, Lord Stamfordham, to request that the word "Regis" be added to the town's name.

Regal and *bog* are words not often used in the same sentence.

The king, obviously not impressed with the place, responded by muttering, "Bugger Bognor," which was his royal prerogative but extremely rude nevertheless. Lord Stamfordham went back to the petitioners and told them, "The king has been graciously pleased to grant your request."

King George was unfair, because Bognor is actually very pleasant in the summer. As a boy, I spent some happy summer breaks there with my grandmother, who lived close to the town. But my fond memories don't change the fact that there's nothing quite so dreary as a British seaside resort in the depths of winter.

I pulled up the collar of my overcoat in a vain attempt to keep dry, as wind and rain pummeled the town's promenade. The fish-and-chips shops were dark, boarded up for the winter season. If you want food, kindly come back in six months.

The frigid sea was dirty grey, and piles of seaweed were strewn around the stony beach, which was deserted save for one brave, mad dog owner, his pet jumping around his feet as if in protest at their walk.

Penny-slot arcades, their garish lights still blinking hopefully, were mostly empty. A few lonely souls, mostly the elderly, woodenly fed coins into slot machines, almost dutifully. They wore faces of those doing time rather than having fun.

I walked to the old pier, a jetty that once extended out a thousand feet into the sea. A century ago, visitors could hand over a penny and stroll out to enjoy the views. Built in the Victorian era, it once boasted a theatre that seated 1,400 people, a bandstand, and a dozen stores. A roof-garden cafe was a popular place where refined souls gathered to sip tea.

But the once-glorious pier is now a shadow of its former self. Battered by storms in 1964 and then again in 1999, most of the pier, including the theatre and the stores, has been washed away by the sea. Now it is a broken skeleton of what it once was, a quick stroll to nowhere. The jetty is now just 350 feet long, where it comes to an abrupt end.

It's estimated that it will take $3 million to restore it, and nobody has the will or the resources for that. And so now all that remains is an amputee pier. At the entrance, yet another penny arcade, an ice cream kiosk, and a small nightclub above the arcade.

As I walked around, all except the arcade were bolted and locked with rusty padlocks. Decay hovered in the air.

I sat down on a set of wooden steps beside the pier, stared out to sea, and imagined the grand pier in its heyday. Once it had staked its claim over the sea, marching proudly out across the turbulent waters, its mighty iron supports seemingly impervious to the elements. Once it had teemed with excited theatregoers, streaming back in their hundreds from the late show, enjoying the glow of thousands of lights that bejeweled a thousand feet of decking.

It had all been swept away—only a broken, useless carcass offers a hint of what used to be. And as I looked out to sea and pondered the rusting, broken pier, I wondered what would become of my faith;

once so firm, so seemingly impervious to assault and erosion, would it end in ruins too?

• • •

The night I became a Christian was the most exhilarating night of my young life. As I hurried home to tell my parents, my heart was full of hope, my head swimming with possibilities.

I had become a Christian.

I was brand new.

Born again.

Everything was different.

Me. A Christian. I could hardly believe that I—a most unlikely candidate for Christianity—was a believer.

My church experience had been limited to being christened as a child—most East London parents had their children "done" in those days—and a couple of visits to Sunday school. As a young teen, I had been openly hostile to faith, sometimes mocking friends who went to church. As a high school student, I worked part-time cleaning trains and gave the one Christian on the crew a terribly hard time.

Faith seemed illogical and ridiculous to me. I wanted to be a rock star, which was unlikely, seeing as I could only play about thirty chords on the guitar. Make that twenty. But I was certain that religion would have no place in my life. Faith was for the weak.

Childhood was a lonely time. I was born to two good, hard-working parents who nevertheless were trying to come to terms with marriage in post-war Britain. My brother married when I was twelve and quickly emigrated to South Africa. I felt quite alone.

My loneliness is best illustrated by the robbery that took place at my family home. The place was turned over while I was in the house. Drawers were opened, the contents scattered. But here's the odd thing. Nothing was taken. The police were called, and I gave them a statement. But the burglar was never found, and the case remains unsolved.

That's a relief, seeing as the intruder was me. I staged a burglary at my own house just to get some attention.

Growing up, I spent my life doing as little as possible to get by at school and being the first person to be absolutely and immediately drunk at parties. I accomplished this by pouring a potentially deadly cocktail of spirits into a pint glass, and drinking it dry in one gulp. It's amazing I didn't die from alcohol poisoning.

The only time I would ever show even the vaguest interest in God was if I went into a church building. I remember that I would furtively cross myself, a cursory nod in the general direction of the Almighty, and a superstitious act with as much depth as making a wish or hoping my path wouldn't be crossed by a black cat. If there was a God—even if he wanted to know me—I had no interest in an introduction.

All that changed, however, when I met Mrs. Richardson.

A religious-education teacher and a minister's wife, she clearly liked me. She had a radiant, beaming smile and an irrepressible faith. Always under pressure, she bustled around the school halls with a pile of unmarked work in her arms. I was simply so intrigued by her that I wanted to please her and so chose her subject as one of my study electives. Sometimes she would talk about Jesus as if he were her friend, but while I admired her, her chatter about her Jesus didn't make any sense to me. The others in the class were all pleasant and somewhat nerdy Christians, and I had no plans to join their gang. But that all changed when a casual prayer of mine was answered in a rather stunning way, one that even I couldn't ignore.

It's all rather embarrassing.

I experienced a rather domestic healing, and telling its story certainly won't produce a bestseller. I was not cured of cancer, and I didn't step out of a wheelchair. I didn't reach out and touch a television screen, make a pledge to donate to someone's ministry, or fall to the ground at the touch of an evangelist's hand.

As an avid swimmer, I'd collected a number of plantar warts on my right foot.

Yep. That's right. Foot warts.

I was about to go to the hospital as a day patient for a minor surgery when, alone in my bed at home, I decided to try praying. Mild fear rather than faith fueled my prayer.

I'm allergic to most forms of pain, hence the stab at prayer, which was more like a hopeful wish upon a faraway star, a request put before the divine tooth fairy. I certainly didn't anticipate any response.

If you're up there, can you take away these foot warts? Amen.

And that was that. Nothing happened. No angels sang. There were no tingles in my foot. No overwhelming sense of any heavenly presence. But by the next morning, they were gone. All gone. Vanished. Someone had taken away my warts.

I called Mrs. Richardson immediately and breathlessly told her what had happened. She invited me to attend the church service that her pastor husband was leading that night. Some people were being baptized, but I had no idea what that was about. As I walked into the church that evening with Ian, a school friend I invited for company (and possible protection), I couldn't know that I was just seconds away from the most significant juncture of my life.

Life turns on a moment or a minute, and that night my life turned 180 degrees.

I was bemused by the worship, intrigued by the preacher, and bewildered by the small swimming pool at the front of the church.

Pastor Richardson, a kindly chap with a broad smile and an infectious laugh, clambered down into the tank, dressed in a long black gown, which immediately ballooned up in the water. His gait was awkward as he gingerly navigated the steps, because he was wearing fisherman's waders that climbed to his thighs. Later a rumor circulated in the youth group that these waders had sprung a small leak, causing him to speed up the proceedings. I'm not sure it's true.

After a brief testimony, each candidate filed down into the tank, one by one. I couldn't believe my eyes as I witnessed what looked like an aquatic mugging. More bewildered than moved by the event, I decided that this religious malarkey was definitely not for me. I nudged my friend, indicating that we needed to get out of this strange place — now. We fled and sat outside in my car. Lighting a cigarette, I cursed repeatedly, then swore that I'd never darken the doors of another church for the rest of my life. Who cared about those disappearing warts?

**&^%! Those people were *&%^5 crazy!

And then, my curse-riddled but solemn vow made, I discovered that I'd left my coat back inside the church. I was going to have to go back in there to retrieve it.

That's the only reason I'm a Christian today.

I forgot my coat.

Gingerly we crept back in, hoping to grab the coat and run, but we were intercepted by David, the youth leader, who seemed jolly well to the point of being slightly scary. Apparently the young people of the church stayed behind after the service to sing songs, share testimonies, and drink cups of tea. The ebullient chap asked us if we'd like to go along.

Right. I wanted to go to that meeting about as much as I wanted an amputation, but I didn't want to disappoint this incredibly kind man. So we agreed, went in, grabbed a cup of tea, sat down, and it was then that one of the baptismal candidates, Malcolm — he was grinning too — approached me and, after the briefest greeting, asked me if I was a Christian. My response was illogical, but typical.

"Of course I'm a Christian; I'm British."

Strangely, most British people used to believe that they were

Christian simply because of being British. It's the sour fruit of believing that you live in something called a "Christian country," as if countries could be Christian. Of course, we Brits are not alone in this mistaken belief.

But even as that nationalistic profession of faith tumbled from my lips, I suddenly, absolutely knew that I was not a Christian at all. Malcolm, earnest and gentle, apologized for any offense his question might have caused. But I cut him short because for no rational reason that I could think of then, I knew that I wanted to be a Christian. I told the now-confused Malcolm that I was sorry, but I had just realized that I needed to make the big step.

I turned and looked at Ian, expecting a "have you lost your mind?" expression. He nodded.

"Me too," he said.

"What do we have to do?" I asked.

An ecstatic look took over Malcolm's face as he realized that on this, the night of his baptism, he was about to lead two young men to Christ. He could hardly contain himself, but his next words were daunting.

"You need to come to the little room at the back of the church."

That sounded scary. It wasn't.

In that little room, beside the dripping ministerial waders hanging on the wall, we heard the greatest news that there has ever been: the gospel.

We knelt down, side by side, and invited Jesus to be our friend, Lord, Savior, and mentor.

The earth didn't shake. No distant birds burst into song. But moments later, when we stood up, somehow I knew that something, maybe even everything, was different.

I'd only gone back for my coat.

I got an invitation to a new life.

I opened the door of the little prayer room expecting to find an empty building. Surely the meetings would be over by now. But word had got around. There were pagans in the house, wanting to become Christians. Every one of those young people waited behind to welcome us into the family of God. As I opened that door and Ian and I stepped out, a great cheer went up.

Incredibly, they formed a long line that went all the way to the back of that building. Ian and I went down that line, receiving hugs and handshakes and hearty congratulations.

When I got off of my knees in the little prayer room, I knew that I was a Christian.

When I got to the back of the line, I knew that I'd found the family of God. At last.

I was home.

It was wonderful.

And utterly bewildering.

• • •

My parents were less than impressed, and I could hardly blame them. For one thing, they'd never heard of a Pentecostal church, so for all they knew, I'd become entangled in a strange cult. My father had been a prisoner of war for four years in World War II until he finally escaped. He'd seen some horrors during battle and then captivity, and struggled to accept that there could be a loving, powerful God at the heart of the universe.

My clumsy and even aggressive attempts to convert him didn't help. He was probably terrified that his youngest son was turning into a religious maniac. Ultimately, both of my parents would come to faith, but that was to come many years later and had little to do with my earnestness; in fact, they probably found Christ despite my efforts, not because of them.

I quickly distanced myself from the group that had helped me stay sane during high school, viewing them as a potentially bad influence. Years later, when we finally got together for a reunion and began to rebuild relationships that had been abandoned four decades earlier, they told me that I had been the bad boy in the group prior to my conversion. I was the one who would try daring and rebellious things first, and then I'd challenge them to take the foolish leap and follow me. But back then, as a new Christian, they were "of the world," and I suddenly was not. I viewed them as a threat, and they had to go. Instead, I immersed myself in building "edifying" friendships with other Christians. Just about every time the doors of the church were open, I was there.

The welcome line that had spontaneously formed the night I became a Christian became significant in more ways than one. Three minutes after I found Christ, I met Kay in that line. She thought my friend Ian was the cute one, but I won. She was just fourteen but was ultimately to become my wife. We've been married for thirty-five years, and she's still the kindest person I've ever met.

I was desperate to be a 100 percent follower of Christ, and wanted to hold no part of my life back from him. And within just a few weeks, I received a dramatic call into full-time Christian ministry.

Everything was shaping up rather well.

· · ·

I'd only been a believer for a matter of days, and now I was beginning to sense a vocational call to leadership. It was crazy.

What does a call look and feel like? How do you know?

Perhaps it's a repeated notion, an idea that at first seems quite incredible, but one that just won't go away. It's fantastic, implausible, but repetitive.

Or it might be a rumbling desire that comes from deep within us, that gnaws away at us with a good intensity.

Or is a call to ministry birthed as we daydream about what it might be like—preaching, caring, leading, and helping people?

Something was happening within me that I couldn't explain—a building sense of excitement about the risk, the adventure, delight about the sense of purpose, yet a sense of being sobered by the cost involved.

And then I went off on a youth retreat weekend, which was being led by a guest speaker from another church, a stranger to most of us. His name was John Barr.

Another juncture moment for me was just around the corner.

• • •

On the opening night of the weekend, I sensed a strange atmosphere, the mingling of anticipation and fear. What did God want to do in our lives? Pastor Barr stood up to deliver his first sermon and told us that he was excited to be involved with the retreat and that he already knew that God was going to do some great things.

That sounded good to me, in a general sense. But then John got specific.

Very specific.

"On my way here," he continued, "while I was driving along, God spoke to me and told me the first and last names of three of you, three young people that he is calling into full-time leadership. This will not be total news to you but will serve as confirmation of what God is already doing inside of you. I'll be chatting with you more over the weekend."

With that, he launched into his opening sermon, but I wasn't really listening—and it wasn't because I thought that I might be one of the three. On the contrary, despite what I had been sensing, it didn't occur to me that I could be chosen like this. And so while John preached away, I spent the time looking around the room, speculating about who the lucky three might be.

Why didn't it occur to me that I might be one of them?

The answer to that question is important, for it's the reason we can spend much of our lives feeling anxious. We can be quick to count ourselves in if there is news of judgment and punishment, but rush to count ourselves out if there is an announcement of blessing, purpose, or calling. And so I counted myself out. Even as my calling was about to be startlingly confirmed, a distant fog bank was forming too.

• • •

On the second night of the retreat, halfway through the worship service, I began to feel like a weighty blanket was being draped over me, a heaviness that was literally pushing me down. I was battling to stay seated upright, and I felt completely bewildered. What on earth was going on?

During a pause between songs, John Barr stood up and said he sensed that the Lord was doing something specific with one of us. He then described — in exact detail — what I was feeling. Was this guy some kind of psychic? After a few minutes, the heavy sensation faded, and I began to wonder if I had imagined the whole experience. An hour later, the service over, I approached John to ask him a question about what had happened. A small line of eager teenagers was waiting to talk with him. I waited my turn.

When I stepped up, I did not introduce myself but just said that what he'd described had been happening to me.

He spoke kindly, just a few sentences of reassurance, and I thanked him and turned to go.

And that's when it happened.

He touched my shoulder lightly and said, "Excuse me, son, . . . but your name is Jeff Lucas, isn't it?"

I froze.

"Er . . . yes, it is, sir."

John smiled.

"You're one of the three that I mentioned last night. God has been calling you into ministry, hasn't he?"

I nodded, dumbstruck.

He smiled again but was obviously unwilling to say more than he had heard.

"Well, get on with it then, son. Get on with it."

I cried myself to sleep that night. God knew my name. I'd known that intellectually in the few weeks that I'd been a Christian, but now I knew it experientially. He knew me. He'd called me. That much was clear.

• • •

But so much still wasn't clear.

In those early months of discipleship, I wanted to fit in with my new friends, to belong, and to even excel as a Christian. Our motives are always mixed, but I don't think that this was just about looking good or appearing to be "spiritual." I was genuinely desperate to please God. But zeal can be hijacked and often is.

What began with passion became pathological—and there's a huge difference between the two. Although my outward behavior seemed balanced enough, inside I was edging into manic extremism. My previous tendencies toward obsessive-compulsive behaviors began to emerge in my spirituality, disguised as commitment and death to self. I had been an agitated, uptight, obsessive unbeliever. Now I was becoming an agitated, uptight, obsessive Christian.

I didn't think for a moment that my past had any bearing on my present. I took Paul's words to heart: "Therefore, if anyone is in Christ, the new creation has come: The old has gone, the new is here!"

Surely I was a new creature in Christ, was I not, so what bearing could my former life have?

But with those words, Paul was making a positional statement about what Christ has done, not suggesting that I was totally renewed the instant I became a Christian. Transformation comes from a lifetime as an apprentice of Christ, not in an instant because of a sinner's prayer prayed. But I did not know that then.

I fretted endlessly because I found prayer to be a chore, and extended times of worship were a challenge (they still are). The songs we sang implied that fellowship with God was easy, natural, and delightful. But my mind would wander when I tried any kind of disciplined prayer, and when the worship leader insisted that we sing that song just one more time, I despaired. Everybody else seemed ecstatic. I found it tiresome. Then as we obediently sang the song for the tenth time, the enthusiastic but repetitive worship leader breathlessly whispered into the microphone, "Do you know, heaven's going to be just like this! Only longer!"

I smiled and nodded but inwardly groaned. I felt horrible. Surely I wouldn't find it boring to be with someone that I was supposed to love, would I? My conclusions were simplistic and dangerous: Perhaps I didn't love God at all.

Someone said that prayer was just like a conversation. "Just talk to Jesus like a close friend," they insisted, "and he will talk back to you." One or two of those around me apparently had so many revelations that it seemed that God was quite chatty—but not with me.

I had experienced the epic encounter with Johnny Barr. God knew my name and had given me a clear call, so I knew that he was and is the God who still speaks. But there was not much ongoing day-to-day conversation with me, or so it seemed. But instead of asking for clarity, instead of interrogating the easy clichés, I sank deeper and deeper into profound shame because I wasn't hearing God. Prayer as conversation? I'd say my piece and then wait for the response: a whisper, a hint, a nudge, a sense of something, or even a voice.

Nothing.

What desperate sin had I committed that was making communication so difficult? And would I know if there was some kind of spiritual blockage in my life? I learned that the heart is desperately wicked and that we are easily self-deceived. Perhaps that was what was happening to me: I was a reprobate but just didn't know it.

The fog thickened.

Now, stuck in endless circles of self-flagellation, I couldn't break out of the pattern. I didn't know then that there are special pitfalls reserved by Satan for the new Christian who is so desperate to do the right thing that he or she easily embraces shame and even despair.

The Bible was a total mystery to me. I had absolutely no idea how the components of Scripture fit together. To make things worse, the only Bible that was widely available back then was the King James Version, and as a seventeen-year-old living in the 1970s, I was frantically trying to make sense of life with a book written in four-hundred-year-old, antiquated language. *The Living Bible* had just been published, but that was viewed with deep suspicion by some of my peers because it is a paraphrase.

It was then that a kindly friend unwittingly gave me some terrible advice. I had confessed that God did not seem to be speaking to me, and so he shared his own approach to hearing God.

"It's easy, Jeff. Just pray about the issue that's on your mind, ask God to speak, and then throw open your Bible and randomly put your finger on any verse. That will be God's answer to your question."

This "pick a blessing" approach was being encouraged by the sale of "promise boxes" in Christian bookstores: cardboard boxes each containing a hundred little scrolls with scriptural promises printed on them; one picked out a promise each day, a scriptural lucky dip. The creators of the promise box probably never intended that they should be used this way, but as far as I was concerned, the use of them endorsed this idea that randomly selecting Scripture verses was a legitimate way to hear from God.

This blatant misuse of Scripture was disastrous. I was dating Kay at the time and was already feeling guilty about the fact that I really liked her (more about that momentarily). Desperate to know if she was "the one," I prayed fervently, threw open my leather-bound King James Bible, and plunged my finger onto the silky, gold-edged page, which landed on Proverbs 2:

> When wisdom entereth into thine heart, and knowledge is pleasant unto thy soul....
>
> To deliver thee from the strange woman, even from the stranger which flattereth with her words;
>
> Which forsaketh the guide of her youth, and forgetteth the covenant of her God.
>
> For her house inclineth unto death, and her paths unto the dead.
>
> None that go unto her return again, neither take they hold of the paths of life....

Beware the prostitute.

It seems ridiculous now, but I really thought that God was talking to me. I obviously didn't think that Kay was actually earning a living as a lady of the night, not least because she was scrupulous in her morality. But paranoia and spiritual intensity together can stir a vivid imagination.

Was God telling me that this might happen in the future, that she would eventually abandon "the covenant of her God," and "forsake the guide of her youth"? Was this a prophetic warning? If it was and I ignored it, would Kay lead me away from the pathway of life, never to return again?

It didn't take long (about six horrendous months) for me to discover that this was a ridiculous approach to the Bible, but by then a more subtle confusion had descended upon my mind.

I heard someone say that there were no such things as coinci-

dences, that everything that happens, however insignificant, is ultimately governed by God. So follow my twisted logic:

There are no coincidences — everything happens by design.
Therefore everything that happens ultimately means something:
if it is planned, then it has significance. Now if I am asking God
about an issue, and my Bible reading for that day has anything that
could be remotely connected to that issue, no matter how much
of a stretch is involved, then my conclusion has to be that God is
speaking to me through the coincidence, because there is no such
thing as a coincidence. Everything is, as someone said at the time,
a "God-incidence."

As you might imagine, this tangled me in even more knots. I'd
read about an issue in my Bible, someone would randomly mention that concept the next day in a casual conversation or during
the sermon on Sunday, and I would dive into yet another desperate
introspective trip to discern what God might be saying.

But it was all to get much, much worse.

Another friend gave me some advice about how I could know
the will of God. The issue of guidance and knowing God's will is one
that many Christians feel anxious about, and it's no overstatement
to say that I nearly had a breakdown in my desperation to know,
for sure, that I was doing what God wanted. My friend's advice was
simplistic: "Jeff, we're called to die to the flesh, to crucify our own
desires and wishes daily, to say, 'Not my will, but yours be done,' like
Jesus did in the garden of Gethsemane."

Then came the knockout punch.

"So it stands to reason that the will of God for your life is probably the thing that you'd least like to do."

This negative approach to guidance is actually very prevalent:
"Don't say you don't want to be a missionary, because if God hears
you say that, then he's going to make you go to India." Or as one

refrigerator magnet puts it—one found in a lot of Christian kitch-ens—"If you want to make God laugh, tell him your plans."

Sounds quite spiritual, but it's warped, twisted thinking.

Of course God knows best. And there are times when our wishes conflict with his purposes, and we need to align ourselves with him and submit. But would I go out of my way to force my children to do the exact opposite of what they hoped for, not because their choice is wrong or hurtful, but because I'd just like to dash their dreams? Would I mock their ideas and aspirations? Would I dismiss their ambitions with a sneer?

But I bought the idea—and that created an immediate problem.

By now I was in love with Kay—and in emotional turmoil because of that love. If the will of God was what I didn't want, then it seemed terribly logical that I had a problem. How could I possibly marry Kay, because I really wanted to marry her? Surely I should find someone that I found quite undesirable and pay the ultimate sacrificial price. I was in total turmoil.

Traumatized, I dashed down to the local Christian bookstore to find a book about guidance. (Having first prayed about which book on the will of God that it was the will of God for me to read. Phew.)

Far from helping, the book compounded my fears. It said that if I was in the perfect will of God, peace would confirm my decisions. But I obviously had no peace, because I was neurotically worried and teetering close to a nervous breakdown.

I was trapped in a circle of despair. I couldn't find peace because I didn't already have peace.

Never mind that the book was effectively teaching that my emotions were the final arbiter in any decision and that the biblical basis for this idea was that the peace of God would act like a "sporting umpire" in my decisions—even though the scriptural passage they cited is about interpersonal relationships and not subjective approaches to guidance.

But I didn't know that back then.

What nearly finished me off was the idea that there is only one perfect partner in the world for a Christian to marry—"the one." These days I realize that this is both theologically bankrupt and philosophically untenable. While God may help engineer the coming together of two people, the notion that one person is the only available candidate for marriage is not supported in Scripture and is practically unworkable. What happens if one of the partners dies, or there is a biblical divorce and a remarriage occurs? Is the new partner a reserve who was kept waiting in the wings? And what if "the one" that I was supposed to marry misses God's will and marries someone else? Does that mean that I am condemned to a "second best" relationship for the rest of my life through no fault of my own? I was worried that I might topple off the terrifying tightrope that was the will of God and end up married to a "two" or worse.

I spent my last two years as a teenager as a smiling follower of Jesus, genuinely glad I had made the decision to follow him. But at the same time, I spent those years—and quite a few more—endlessly fretting, anxious, always asking God for more direction, more confirmation. I responded at every service, regardless of what the sermon was about. I'd be the first to raise my hand in guilty response, the first to rush to the front to tearfully ask for prayer. My pastor was amazingly patient and unfailingly kind, but even his wise counsel couldn't shake me out of my angst.

I began to wonder if my friends were really experiencing God in the way they said they were. But I buried my worries by saying that the problem was with me, not them. Even on my wedding day, which should have been so happy, I fretted that perhaps my bride was too beautiful, that I had been wayward in my choice. Our wedding night was a religious event in the worst possible way.

My mother was in the hospital and so had been unable to attend the wedding. After the reception, we drove to London to visit her;

Kay put her wedding dress on again, and we went into the ward and spent some time at her bedside. She was delighted. But it was 2:00 a.m. when at last we reached the little cottage that we had borrowed from my grandmother for the first few days of our honeymoon. We were exhausted. But nuptial bliss was not the first item on the agenda. Although it was the middle of the night, we spent some time reading the Bible and praying together. The next morning we got up and went to church. I was asked to give a testimony (a little challenging after one's wedding night), then we went to the pastor's home for tea. And then it was back to the evening service. Our honeymoon was packed with passionate singing.

At first glance, this devotion to prayer, Bible study, and church attendance seems like it was in part a genuine desire to put the Lord Jesus first in our lives, and especially in our marriage. There was something quite beautiful about those decisions.

But there were deeper, darker reasons for our apparent dedication. Our honeymoon devotions were also due in part to my neuroses; I was trying to justify our faltering steps into the land of eros with as much spiritual activity as possible. We didn't pray, read the Bible, and go to church services on our honeymoon just because we wanted to—we went because I had to. I needed to keep a smile on God's face. Or at least try to bring a smile to his face.

. . .

Five years passed. As a young married couple now in full-time ministry, we planted a church on a housing estate in the English midlands. It was a success; the handful of people we began with grew to just under a couple hundred. We then built a worship center and a day nursery center, and helped plant another congregation. God was answering our prayers, and even with all of my unresolved confusion, there was an uncluttered simplicity to our faith.

When we sought to buy a piece of land for our new church

building, we were firmly told that there was no way: the lot was on a prime spot right at a major junction in the city, and the council didn't want a church building there. And so I had assembled our little congregation on that lot, and we marched around it and prayed, Jericho-style. No walls or buildings fell down, it being bare land, but the next week the city council informed us that we could have the land after all—as long as we were willing to pay only 25 percent of its value because we were a charity.

Delighted, we obviously agreed.

Life was busy. By now, Kay and I had one child, another on the way, and had fostered two teenage children. I'd been working two full-time jobs, delivering milk, as well as leading the church. Money was short because we'd built the church building.

I was also deeply depressed and on medication. I had to abandon the milk delivery job because I was suffering from hypertension. And so I continued my more-than-full-time role as a pastor and told few people about my "black dog," as Churchill tagged his depression.

I felt bad.

And I felt bad because I felt bad.

Where was the joy that I was preaching about? Was I a complete hypocrite? I was sad and deeply ashamed of my sadness. I mistakenly thought that my feelings were the barometer of my spirituality.

It certainly wasn't all grim; I'd grown out of some of my madder notions. Five years had taught me that some of what I'd believed in the early stages of faith was ridiculous spiritual quackery—but trying to separate what was true and substantial from what was illusionary was confusing. Sifting through it all was both difficult and frightening.

Our theology is both defined and instinctive; there are certain truths that we believe with clarity, and yet we still respond emotionally according to how life has conditioned us. So I knew intellectually that the grace of God was amazing and accepting, but emotionally

I was still nervous, even cowering at times. There were also special challenges that came because my faith was of the Pentecostal charismatic kind. I genuinely wanted to experience the voice and activity of the Holy Spirit in the congregation that I led. But while I believed that the gift of speaking in and the interpretation of tongues is contemporary for today (and still do), I wrestled with a pastoral question: Was God really inspiring what some of our congregation shared during our meetings? Usually the same person shared each week, and the interpretations were offered in King James language—was this God speaking?

And it wasn't just that I was anxious about others. It was me that I was most suspicious of. What about the "prayer language" that I used in private prayer? I had been told that it was the gift of tongues again. But while I had no doubts about that gift being fully available today, was what I had the real thing, or was I just jabbering away, making it all up? It certainly sounded rather ridiculous.

And then I was becoming disappointed by the larger church scene. When anyone stepped out of line by asking difficult questions about doctrine, there were those who swiftly rushed in like self-appointed Christian "thought police," eager to punish any noncompliance. Christians may not use guns, but they often assault each other with labeling machines. Someone asks a question or honestly expresses their struggle with doubt or admits to a concern about a doctrine that in turn creates controversy, and the label-slapping begins.

Liberal. Doubter. Even heretic.

Honest conversation is rendered impossible, and ironically, the truth seems less true, because some are terrified of interrogating their beliefs with unsettling but necessary questions. Suddenly faith seems flimsy.

What are they so afraid of?

For me, the plague of questions was growing. Sometimes I'd

wake up in the night, fearing that I was drowning in the dark. In the lonely sleepless hours, I feared hell.

Mildly claustrophobic, I woke up in a cold sweat a few times and then lay there, staring at the dim ceiling, wrestling with the thought that hell for me would be being buried alive, a wooden coffin lid pressing my nose down. I even worried that if God was as angry as some made him sound, he might consign me to that coffin, a fate worse than death, because it would last forever. Loving such a God was rather difficult.

At times I couldn't make my mind up about what would be worse — if the gospel was true, then that left me with a million questions, and if it were all false, then I'd been giving my life for nothing, my youth sacrificed for a lost cause.

I began to think the unthinkable.

The church is a very effective prison. You come in because you're damned if you don't.

You can't leave because the threat of damnation is still out there if you wander or walk away.

Leaders tell you what to do, apparently authorized by God to do so.

You hand over at least 10 percent of your income, and if you don't, the inference — sometimes clear, sometimes implied — is that God will be mad at you if you don't write the check, and he'll curse your finances.

As I dug deeper and meandered around the mysterious caverns of my heart and mind, I discovered that there were times when, unconsciously, I didn't actually want people to become Christians — not a great conclusion for a church planter.

Then there were the relational struggles that come to every leader. With experience, ministers learn to navigate through seasons when the spotlight of criticism is placed on them, but I was very young. Most of the congregation were generous and kind to a fault, but there were some notable exceptions, including one man who would turn his chair toward the wall while I was preaching to let me know that he was not listening to me. It was unfortunate that he was also a deacon. When a few Christians acted like predators with razor-sharp teeth, I worried about our efforts at evangelism—I didn't want to have a hand in creating one more unkind zealot armed with a Bible and "a mission from God."

God seemed specially chatty with a few. One or two of the more enthusiastic souls in our flock seemed just a little disjointed, tilted into oddness by their faith. Did I really want to lead someone else into that potential twilight zone of weirdness if they embraced the way of discipleship?

Christianity seemed so utterly impossible. I was weary of traveling but never arriving. I was sick of spending my days shoved around by a barrage of insistent oughts, shoulds, and should-nots. I plunged into secret despair, but word got out to a few. Then, when they finally heard that I was battling depression, some of my friends were not helpful.

I discovered that the book of Job teaches us that when you're exhausted and ready to give up, well-meaning people show up with ridiculous advice and then tell you that they're speaking on behalf of God.

So we hear that you haven't got the victory.

Apparently not.

What can we do to sort you out? (Some well-meaning Christians are on an endless safari to sort out everyone around them.)

I bristled inwardly and thought, *How can you help me? How about going away forever? That'd be a great start.* But I kept my mouth shut.

I still really wanted to walk by faith with the real Jesus, but the road ahead seemed daunting, foggy, and deeply uncertain. In trying to unravel my thoughts and sift the truth from the myths, the worrying question haunted me: Would I have anything left?

I walked down under the pier, kicking pebbles as I crunched my way across that cold, unyielding beach. I stood and stared up at those rust-ravaged, once-strong Victorian supports, and I wondered, was my faith just like that pier, once bright and hopeful, now ravaged by storms? Broken beyond repair?

3

• • •

BEHOLD,
I COME QUIETLY

So they went out and got into the boat, but that night they caught
nothing. Early in the morning, Jesus stood on the shore, but the
disciples did not realize that it was Jesus.

JOHN 21:3 – 4

Somehow, in the midst of our tears, a gift is given. Somehow, in
the midst of our mourning, the first steps of a dance take place.
Somehow, the cries that well up from our losses belong to our
song of gratitude.

HENRI J. M. NOUWEN

We are here to abet creation and to witness it, to notice each
thing so each thing gets noticed. Together, we notice not only the
mountain shadow and each stone on the beach, but we notice
each other's beautiful face and complex nature so that creation
need not play to an empty house.

ANNIE DILLARD

As the shadows lengthened and the early evening sun dipped lower, the disciples headed for the boat that most likely belonged to Peter—hence the term *the boat*. Peter knew every inch of that boat of his. Nighttime was best for fishing in Galilee, as the surplus of the catch could be sold first thing the next morning. They'd have full stomachs and full pockets.

Besides, fishing would be the perfect therapy.

For the last three years, they'd all spent so much time grasping for what often seemed intangible, wrestling with Jesus' confusing statements, sometimes seeing the point of his parabolic tales immediately, but other times totally missing the message. Some days they felt like kings—and on others, like bumbling fools.

Without Jesus with them day and night as he had been, there was a leadership vacuum. They'd become used to following, and Peter emerged as a natural leader.

So when he took the initiative and announced his fishing plan, the others readily agreed. They had their favorite spots to trawl. They'd enjoy the familiar, rough feel of the rope nets, the gentle swaying of the boat, the firm grip of the oars, the camaraderie and banter.

The five on that particular trip named in Scripture were all from Galilee, and if the two unnamed were Andrew and Philip, then this was the Galilean Seven. But it turned out to be an exhausting exercise in futility. A pleasant evening morphed into a long night. They'd trawled again and again, back and forth, but each time they hauled up a totally empty net. The gospel writer John crafts his language carefully to emphasize the frustration: they caught nothing.

Zero.

Zilch.

No breakfast, no bounty.

Cue somber, maybe eerie music for this scene. Play minor chords because the atmosphere was undoubtedly heavy.

When John tells us that all this happened at night, this is more than a time check. In his gospel, he uses darkness like an artist with a color palette, painting the mood in funeral hues. Nicodemus used the cover of night to come to Jesus by stealth, and Judas deserted Jesus under the same canopy of darkness. Resurrection morning was shrouded in darkness, and at nighttime the disciples huddled behind locked doors because they were desperately afraid.

Look at those tired and agitated fishermen, halfheartedly casting the net yet again, sighing as they did so — let's try one more time — somehow knowing it was a waste of time. Did they know before the sodden nets were even hauled up for the umpteenth time that it was a foregone conclusion? Empty again.

And then, in that hour before dawn, when the still-submerged sun gives but a hint of its impending ascent, they were trawling about a hundred yards from the shore. Peering through the morning mist, they realized that someone was just standing there on the beach, watching them.

Who is he?

What's he doing there, alone, so early, on the beach?

Why does he stare at us so?

The experiences of the last couple of weeks taught them that, in life, anything could happen. The sight of a staring stranger might seem menacing, especially when you're sleep deprived.

• • •

There's something about this scene that has bothered me for years, but I couldn't identify it until recently. Every Bible commentator rushes to the moment when Jesus appears to rescue his friends, help with their fishing, and cooks that life-changing breakfast. He saves the hour, and the day. And then I realized what was niggling me.

He let them work all night.

They spent hours of frustration that likely distilled to despair. Hard labor that produced nothing but aching backs. Sleep squandered on a lost cause. And then he arrived. He could have shown up seven hours earlier when they began their jaunt and helped them at the outset. But they were abandoned to a dark night before he intervened in the early morning. Did he stand back for a reason, perhaps allowing them to attend a seven-hour class on dependency? Was his distance deliberate, creating a space to nudge them into understanding before he finally stepped in?

He'd done that before, during those amazing three years. He allowed them to panic just a little when the thousands who were following him had nothing to eat. A hungry crowd is a difficult beast to tame, but instead of immediately solving the problem, he handed them the problem to solve:

You give them something to eat.

They chattered on about how much that would cost and didn't take the hint, so he stepped back in. A lunch was surrendered, multiplied, and twelve basketfuls were left over, testimony to what Jesus had done and perhaps what the disciples could have done if they'd tried.

He made another attempt after the transfiguration. Having witnessed an epic revelation of his glory and power, the disciples bumped into a man whose son was tormented by a demonic spirit; the symptoms were destructive and the father was in despair. The disciples tried and failed to deliver the boy. At last, succumbing to the complaint of the distressed father, Jesus stepped in, took over and brought deliverance and healing. But he was frustrated by the lack of faith of his hapless apprentices.

What did Jesus want his friends to discover as they muttered and wondered and then hauled up the empty net yet again? Perhaps they needed to discover that fishing would not be their work going forward. As we'll see later, there's a lot of talk about fish and fishing in this episode.

Or was this to teach them that they were called into a life of full partnership with him, that it would be by following his directions that the bumper catch would result? Now, by faith, they were called into a new dependency on him for every area of their lives.

Or maybe they, as professional fisherman, had to learn how to admit abject failure, which would prepare the ground for a really honest conversation following breakfast.

In truth, we'll never know. Perhaps in this case there was no specific outcome intended: everything doesn't have to mean something. There are some lessons that are only learned when God apparently steps back, allowing us to struggle through. But knowing that school might be in session doesn't change the fact that feeling abandoned is a cold, dark, and lonely experience.

• • •

Throughout the big story of Scripture, God is portrayed as the one who appears to abandon his people and then intervenes again, sometimes after years, decades, or even centuries of silence. Martin Luther and Thomas Aquinas called this "deus absconditus," the God who absconds. The fifteenth-century monk Saint John of the Cross famously named those seasons "the dark night of the soul." The prophet Habakkuk wailed that God was ignoring him, turning a deaf ear to his prayers:

> How long, LORD, must I call for help,
>   but you do not listen?

The Psalmist felt the same hollowness of soul and cried out in desperation,

> My God, my God, why have you forsaken me? . . .
> My God, I cry out by day, but you do not answer,

by night, but I find no rest....
But you, LORD, do not be far from me.

Jesus himself felt the loneliness of the human condition, and
perhaps the apparent remoteness of his Father, as he hung upon the
cross:

My God, my God, why have you forsaken me?

As Jesus yelled out those words of the forsaken one, he was quot-
ing Psalm 22, which ultimately concludes with words of praise and
victory. Authentic faith often includes a sense of desertion; prayer
can begin with an honest declaration of despair, because the lonely
pathway of abandonment—or at least the sense that we have been
abandoned—is well trodden. Paul insists that while we might be
persecuted, we are never abandoned by God, and the writer to the
Hebrews assures us of God's promise:

Never will I leave you;
        never will I forsake you.

But actual abandonment and apparent abandonment feel just
the same.
Desolate.

• • •

I was angry that Jesus apparently abandoned me to my youthful
obsessive behavior. Why didn't he sweep in and save me from myself,
like the superhero I supposed him to be? Wasn't I desperately trying
to please him? Couldn't he have sent someone, done something to
lift me out of the years of compulsive behavior that eventually led
me into dark depression? I was obviously not alone in feeling left to
struggle so.

Donald McCullough was a distinguished college president,
author, and celebrated pastor until his sexual infidelity meant that he

was banished in disgrace. McCullough tells of many lonely walks on the beach in his poignant book *The Wisdom of Pelicans*, and describes what felt like desertion by God:

> And speaking of God, where is he? (or she, as the case may be?) I feel abandoned and alone. The moment I say this, I hear a theological professor within me: "You are not alone, not really, for God is present with you even in this mess, and someday you will look back on it as a time of growth." I know this lecture by heart, have it frigging memorized, because I've delivered it many times to poor souls sitting on their own beaches. But soon the lecture is drowned out by something much louder: the silence. Where is God? Who is God?

Abandonment is a recurring theme of McCullough's harrowing journey:

> A question troubles me, takes me by the throat and won't let go. Where is God in all of this? If God is sovereign, why hasn't the divine arm reached down to direct my situation? Why didn't God protect me from my own vulnerabilities, and why hasn't God prevented this mess that seems to be growing like an out-of-control oil spill? I have always trusted that God is on my side, but now I have enough evidence to question this. I don't doubt that God loves me in the most general sense, as in "God so loved the world," but I am finding it hard to believe the part about every hair on my head being numbered. Why has God abandoned me?

Peter Scazzero, the bestselling author of *The Emotionally Healthy Church*, spent eight years church planting in Queens, New York City, but battled with depression and nearly lost his marriage. When his wife finally told him that she wanted to leave their church because she had lost all respect for his leadership and a trusted fellow leader was championing a church split, Scazzero felt the threat of abandonment, and not just from fellow humans:

> The next two years were marked by a slow descent into an abyss. It felt like an infinite black hole was threatening to swallow me. I cried out to God for help, to change me. It seemed as if God closed heaven to my cry rather than answer it. Things went from bad to worse.

Suffering can amplify feelings of abandonment. Despite all our theological and philosophical assertions about the nature of the fallen world we live in and the problem of pain, we instinctively want to believe that a loving Father would intervene and spare us when we are in agony. Elie Wiesel survived the death camps of Auschwitz and Buchenwald, and tellingly describes a Polish rabbi:

> He was a bent old man, whose lips were always trembling. He used to pray all the time, in the block, in the yard, in the ranks. He would recite whole passages of the Talmud from memory, argue with himself, ask questions and answer himself. And one day he said to me: "It's the end. God is no longer with us."
>
> And, as though he had repented of having spoken such words, so clipped, so cold, he added in his faint voice: "I know. One has no right to say things like that. I know. Man is too small, too humble and inconsiderable to seek to understand the mysterious ways of God. But what can I do? I'm not a sage, one of the elect, nor a saint. I'm just an ordinary creature of flesh and blood. I've got eyes too, and I can see what they are doing here. Where is the divine Mercy? Where is God? How can I believe, how could anyone believe, in the Merciful God?

And even those who are dubbed saints, icons of passionate commitment to Christ at great personal cost, are not exempt from seasons when they feel abandoned by or distant from God. Few would question Mother Teresa's dedication as she poured out her life on the fetid streets of Calcutta. Having visited the home for the sick and dying that she founded, I can testify firsthand to the selfless and harrowing work of the Sisters of Mercy. But for most of her life, the diminutive saint couldn't find a sense of God's closeness, "neither in her heart or in the Eucharist." "Jesus has a very special love for you," she wrote, describing the hollowness she felt. "As for me, the silence and the emptiness is so great that I look and do not see, listen and do not hear."

And then, in 1961, she spoke of her unrequited yearning for God:

> Darkness is such that I really do not see—neither with my mind nor with my reason—the place of God in my soul is blank—There is no God in me—when the pain of longing is so great—I just long and long for God.... The torture and pain I can't explain.

Wonderfully, Teresa trudged on, comforting, caring, and loving people in the name of Christ, despite her feelings of emptiness and abandonment. She was not spared her desolation of soul but determined to dance on through the tears. But Teresa kept the depth of her pain a secret. Too many Christians feel irrationally ashamed because of the emotional turbulence that they feel, as if depression is a symptom of a lack of faith. James Martin, an editor at the Jesuit magazine *America* and the author of *My Life with the Saints*, wrote, "I've never read a saint's life where the saint has such an intense spiritual darkness. No one knew she was that tormented."

As a young Christian, my passion for God was tinged with torment. I wish that God had rescued me from my youthful angst. Yet my aloneness was a forge. It drove me to pursue answers rather than passively accept the answers I'd been given. It gave me a hunger and a thirst for truth and vulnerability. I became desperate to find the real Jesus, and that desperation for him continues to this day.

Back then, as I wrestled with legalism, traditionalism, fear, and depression, I learned that questions about faith are not only permissible, but vital. I stumbled upon the discovery that being honest about our struggles liberates others, because all truth, even ugly truth, brings freedom. I learned that God only uses fragile, limping people, because that's the only kind of people there are. I found empathy with the depressed. I learned that life is not about every circumstance being neatly folded around my desires and whims. Alan Jones, dean of Grace Cathedral, San Francisco, wrote, "What we need is a radical sense of exile — separation, distance — if we are to be saved from the illusion that we are at the center of reality."

As the light began to dawn on my night, and some of the fog began to clear and I experienced comfort, so I have been able to comfort others with the comfort that I've received. And if God had apparently gone missing for a while, it was not that I had seen the last of him.

Neither had Peter and his exhausted friends. But when he showed up again, it was not in a way that they might have anticipated. The coming of God is always a surprise, not only because he comes to us, but often because of the manner in which he comes.

• • •

At last Jesus arrived.

Finally.

Was it early morning mist or the half light of the approaching dawn that caused them not to recognize him? It sounds irreverent to say it, but I will, to make a point: Perhaps one of those stick-on name badges would have been useful for the resurrection appearances.

JESUS.

Letters in thick, black marker pen. Unmissable. It would have helped, because after the resurrection, so many people bumped into Jesus without realizing it was him.

The exhausted pair on the Emmaus Road were unaware of whom they were talking to and had a lengthy conversation about their disappointments regarding Jesus—with Jesus. Traditionally it's thought that God himself prevented them from identifying him until bread was broken or that he looked completely different after the Easter event, but the Bible doesn't specify either.

Luke just tells us that "they were kept from recognizing him." The word he uses literally means "their eyes were under arrest." Perhaps a combination of tiredness, disappointment, and a haste to just get home and get some sleep was what blinkered them. When we're exhausted, we don't see straight at all. For whatever reason, they didn't know it was him until, having compelled him to accept their hospitality, they broke bread together.

Another case of mistaken identity occurred when the risen Jesus met the weeping Mary and she mistook him for the gardener. He's the Son of God, newly triumphant over death and hell—and she thought he was the hired help. Was it her tears that blinded her?

Back at the boat, the disciples didn't realize who the stranger on the shore was, even though he was right there, their friend Jesus standing on that beach. I'm relieved. Because if they didn't see straight, then surely there are many times when we won't "see" or sense him too. But were there other reasons for their failure to know that it was really him?

Perhaps they didn't initially recognize him because they didn't expect to see him there. They had been told that he would meet them in Galilee. Despite that, their minds were still cluttered with Jewish traditions and expectations, which included the belief that the

Messiah would come, overthrow the enemies of Israel, and then set up a throne in Jerusalem, sixty-eight miles away.

When Jesus had headed for Jerusalem, James and John requested thrones at his right and left. To their thinking,

Messiah + Jerusalem = thrones

So what would the risen Messiah be doing back in humble Galilee?

Even weeks after this breakfast, following those forty days of kingdom training, they thought he was going to restore the kingdom to Israel. Throne time in Jerusalem again. Perhaps bad ideas were blinding them, stifling any anticipation that he might actually show up.

And then he came so very quietly.

If I'd been asked to choreograph that morning, there would have been no room for doubt about the identity of the stranger on the shore. I would have organized a very different event.

Steven Spielberg on steroids.

Fireworks exploding across the sky, banishing the darkness in a Technicolor cascade.

Hordes of angels belting out the "Hallelujah Chorus" from Handel's *Messiah*, prophetically, because it hadn't been written yet.

Jesus, laughing, striding triumphantly across the waves, an encore performance.

But this was a very ordinary resurrection appearance. He's just standing there. Wordless. Watching. He's there all right.

But he's arrived without fanfare or fuss.

• • •

God didn't abandon me. He's given his word on that to us all. He's pledged his presence, forever and always. But if he was and is with me always, then his appearing in my life and accompanying me hasn't looked like I expected. It was not that I was disappointed with Jesus; it was more that I was disappointed with Jesus as I had imagined he would be. But I shouldn't be surprised that he has not been what I had expected. He usually isn't.

For one thing, after nearly forty years as a Christian, I have yet to be fully, properly introduced to Jesus. That will come one day. The Bible acknowledges that on this side of eternity our vision is impaired. One day we'll see Christ with 20/20 clarity, but in the meantime, our perception of him is skewed, like the reversed image that a mirror offers: "For now we see only a reflection as in a mirror; then we shall see face to face."

We are called to believe in what we cannot see.

I've decided that God being with me does not mean that life will be punctuated daily by stunning revelations. My calling was dramatic: a visiting speaker announcing your name out of the blue and confirming your life vocation is quite the head turner. It was amazing. Wonderful. But because God spoke so loud and clear and did something so dramatic to get my attention, I expected him to keep shouting and that the drama would continue, especially when I had a significant decision to make.

I don't believe that God was the architect of my angst. But he was and is the redeemer of it.

My wing of the larger church — the charismatic Pentecostal crowd — love to emphasize God speaking to us today, a now word. Revelation.

Agreed. God speaks.

But we're not quite so good at recognizing the Bible's emphasis on the development of wisdom, which we grow in not because we hear a voice, but because we learn the lessons that the academy of our daily lives can teach us.

And as I ponder the sight of Jesus, quietly watching his friends as they haul in empty nets once again, I realize that God being with me does not mean that life is endlessly exciting, a hop, skip, and jump from one supernatural experience to another.

But perhaps we are prone to give the impression that it is.

• • •

Worship is dangerous because we instinctively treat the lyrics of the songs we sing as if they carry the same weight as Scripture. After all, we're singing them corporately, and so someone, somewhere, approved them, didn't they?

In worship, we don't just sing to God, but we declare truth to one another, as we speak to each other with "psalms, hymns, and songs from the Spirit." And that means it's vital that we're not serenading each other with myths and half-truths.

Last Sunday, in the singing of just one song, I declared that:

I felt good. But I didn't, because I was bristling at the song and battling a niggling headache.

I felt peace. No, I didn't feel very peaceful, because I didn't feel good, and the song made me anxious about my lack of good feelings, and ...

I felt Jesus in that place. But to be honest, I can't say I consciously felt anything much, never mind the presence of Jesus.

We went on to declare that we could see glory on each face. Admittedly, there were one or two ecstatic looks and some shining eyes, but I wouldn't go so far as to say glory. And some faces were fixed in their usual expression of nonchalant boredom.

Then, incredibly, we proclaimed that we could hear the rustle of angels' wings.

Eh?

Not so.

And if the warriors of the Lord did show up with whooshing wings, I probably wouldn't be singing about it. I'd be alongside everyone else, prostrate on the floor, terrified.

Not only are these words untrue (sorry to be blunt), but they are disempowering. Twelve rows of pews from the worship leader, someone is no doubt worrying that their faith is deficient because they feel bad, anxious, oblivious to any atmosphere or perceived presence of Jesus, unaware of any communal glory. And much as they try, they can't for the life of them hear any rustle of feathers, angelic or otherwise. What they actually feel is excluded.

It's all so unnecessary, because worship is more about who God is than how I feel today. Our emotions don't have to endorse our worship. Our feelings won't always add an amen to the truths we affirm, and that's fine. The gospel is not true only when I feel that it is, and the notion that Christianity is always exciting is a myth. In fact, let me take that further and risk ire as I do so.

Jesus is not always exciting.

Some Christians insist that Jesus is endlessly thrilling. I don't believe it. When Jesus was on this earth, he certainly provided some thrilling episodes. Marble-cold corpses suddenly took possession of a pulse. There was that in-your-face encounter with a screaming demoniac, which led to deliverance for him and drowning for a herd of stampeding pork. Blind eyes blinked and opened—all heady, exhilarating stuff. No, Jesus certainly isn't dull; he is fascinating, intriguing, and endlessly surprising. As Einstein famously said, he is the "luminous Nazarene."

But his friends didn't always find him exciting. His invitation to them to Gethsemane was to an endurance test—one they failed. Life with Jesus frequently got difficult and exhausting. One time the disciples affirmed their commitment to him with a shrug-the-shoulders sigh of resignation: "To whom shall we go? You have the words of eternal life."

We obviously do not walk with Jesus as they did, but rather navigate our days by faith. Yes, there are breakthroughs. Answers to prayer. Episodes that seem to sparkle with divine intervention. But the Bible is clear: faith is not just about miracles, but also the miracle of endurance, when we feel little or nothing.

Being addicted to excitement is immature. If someone said that they were only committed to a marriage as long as it remained exciting, we'd tell them to grow up. But when a Christian says that they're changing churches because their "spiritual thirst is not being satisfied, that they just need more excitement," we bow to their air of spirituality.

We need churches that can be boring, because life often is filled with people who are committed to each other and not just together for the thrills and chills. The truth is that there are days and seasons of "nothing" or "not much." There are times when he comes in such an ordinary, everyday way. And to insist that he only arrive with trumpet and angel song and trembling mountains is to run the risk of missing his fingerprint on the more everyday yet nonetheless beautiful aspects of life. Michael Frost said,

> We have locked God into the so-called sacred realms of church
> and healings and miracles and marvels.... We seem to be try-
> ing so hard to "bring down fire from heaven" in our worship
> services while all along God's favor is to be found in sunshine
> on our faces, the sea lapping at our toes, picking our children
> up at school, or a note from a caring friend.

He arrived that day on a beach in a Galilean backwater. He either went fishing himself that morning or shopping the day before because part of the breakfast was already prepared. And so he comes to us, and he stays with us.

But our experience of him might not be what we think.

4

...

BRINGING AN OFFERING OF NOTHING

He called out to them, "Friends, haven't you any fish?"

"No," they answered.

He said, "Throw your net on the right side of the boat and you will find some." When they did, they were unable to haul the net in because of the large number of fish.

Then the disciple whom Jesus loved said to Peter, "It is the Lord!" As soon as Simon Peter heard him say, "It is the Lord," he wrapped his outer garment around him (for he had taken it off) and jumped into the water. The other disciples followed in the boat, towing the net full of fish, for they were not far from shore, about a hundred yards.

JOHN 21:5 – 8

Nothing in my hand I bring,
simply to the cross I cling.

AUGUSTUS TOPLADY, "ROCK OF AGES"

Our churches are filled with people who outwardly look contented and at peace but inwardly are crying out for someone to love them ... just as they are ... confused, frustrated, often frightened, guilty, and often unable to communicate even within their own families. But the other people in the church look so happy and contented that one seldom has the courage to admit his own deep needs before such a self-sufficient group as the average church meeting appears to be.

KEITH MILLER

Haven't you any fish?"

Try asking that of any fisherman sometime, if you dare.

Stroll up to an angler who has been parked by a lakeside all night. Peer into his bucket or the storage net that dangles from the bank. If you notice that there's no catch, then go ahead, make his day.

"No fish, eh?"

Now put that question to seven irritated, sleep-deprived fishermen, some of whom were professionals, and you're definitely asking for trouble.

Or, as happened when Jesus put the question, you're trying to help your dear friends out of trouble.

I'm not sure what is the greater miracle—the huge catch of fish, right on cue, or the fact that a group of exasperated fishermen took the advice of an inquisitive stranger. When they let the nets down at his instruction, they still didn't know that their self-appointed fishing instructor was Jesus. But for now, look away from the fishermen and ignore the teeming net and all those flapping silver fish—and look at the man on the shore.

A fishing trip was changed when the disciples obeyed a stranger's directions. But the fishermen's lives were utterly changed when they saw the man on the shore with clarity and then shared a meal with him.

Too many of us live tortured, unsatisfying Christian lives because we worship a Jesus who is good at commands but never asks questions; who is a demanding employer but not a caring, tender friend; who asks us to do the unreasonable but never says "well done." What we believe about who God is determines how we'll live. We all have a version of what Jesus is like.

What is your version?

When a person becomes a Christian, he or she doesn't immediately download a balanced, orthodox, coherent understanding of Christ. Our faith is a patchwork quilt, the stitching together of thousands of conversations, fragments from courses we've attended, and chatter we've shared after services.

Preaching and teaching obviously contribute to the way that we perceive God. If we've sat under leadership that is cold, ranting, impersonal, and endlessly demanding, then it stands to reason that this will shape our view of the Lord. We will begin to worship a cold, ranting, impersonal, and endlessly demanding God. Add in our perceptions of God's activity, or non-activity, in our lives. Mingle all of that with the way our upbringing has shaped the way we think about life in general and God in particular, together with our emotional temperament, and we realize that our perception of God is not precise, but is a hotchpotch, a construction.

Picture this, if you will. Imagine that the disciples see a man standing on the beach, his feet spread, his hands on his hips, a gesture of disgust. They peer through the dawn mist, and even from that distance, they feel that he is glowering at them; they sense his disapproval.

His stare is fixed, his eyes cold. Suddenly something erupts in him, and he paces now, just a few steps, back and forth, his fists balled, his back bowed forward in angry tension. He stops and slowly turns and looks out at the boat, straight at them. He cups his hands to his mouth and yells, his voice bellowing across the water, an otherworldly sound. His words are laced with rage.

"Get that boat of yours back here! Now!"

Frantically they grab the oars and pump them as fast as their spent strength will allow. He watches them in silence, the grimace on his face speaking volumes. When they near the beach, his voice is trembling, the anger obvious and barely controlled.

"Just look at you. As soon as you got home, what did you do? You head back to the nets again. So that's how the so-called fishers of men end up. And look at you all. You can't even land some fish in a lake that's teeming ..." He breaks off.

"It's pathetic. You're pathetic."

Is that anywhere close to your perception of God? Does he stand on tiptoe, always on the brink of judgment, finger poised on the smite button? Has he decided not to condemn you for now, because of grace, but you've no idea how long the amnesty will last?

Rather than being hopeful for your success, does he expect you to fail because although you believe in him, he doesn't believe in you?

If that's your Jesus, he's not the same as the Jesus who stood quietly on that beach.

Of course, while Jesus did at times get frustrated with his disciples, the Jesus I worshiped in my earlier years seemed to be always frustrated with me. Whatever I did, I always anticipated the red-pen treatment that my high school teachers gave to my indifferent attempts at homework: C minus. Could do better.

My Jesus back then was eternally unimpressed, his love for me a concession, not a passion. He certainly wasn't into beaches and breakfasts.

• • •

"Friends, haven't you any fish?"

Friends.

I'm glad to say it's a poor translation, because the word doesn't carry the weight or warmth of the word that Jesus used to address that weary group. A better translation is "children" or "lads." The only time that Jesus uses this word in John's gospel, it's both tender and personal, and Jesus' use of it obviously made a lasting impact, especially on John, because he borrowed precisely the same word years later to address a young Christian community:

I am writing to you, dear children ...
    Dear children, this is the last hour ...

Perhaps I missed the stunningly obvious, that the alphabet of
Christianity begins with "f" for father. But I lost sight of the truth
that Jesus sees me as a lad, as a child. It might have been the product
of my becoming a minister at such a very young age. I felt that I had
to be very grown up and responsible from my earliest days of faith.
    Dear children ...
    Children play. They make a huge mess when they paint, often
eating more paint than they put on paper. They misunderstand, ask
endless questions, and giggle a lot.
    My Christianity was the intense, furrowed-brow kind. I talked
earlier about my terror of missing the will of God. I didn't realize
early in my faith that Jesus knew full well that I had the capacity to
not hear or to misinterpret his directions. Even as a new convert, I
couldn't conceive that he saw me as a learning, growing child. I felt
the responsibility to get it right very squarely on my shoulders, and it
was a crushing weight. I repeatedly read that promise of his about his
yoke being easy, and his burden light, and wondered what on earth
he was talking about, because it certainly didn't feel that way to me.
I was desperately trying to be very grown up.
    One of the saddest by-products of gaining so-called maturity is
the loss not of childishness, but of being childlike. Jesus shocked his
disciples by pointing to a child as an example of how to navigate the
kingdom. In a culture that did not cherish or value children as we
do today, this was a stunning idea. Jesus made it clear that it was not
simplicity, innocence, or even just trust that he was celebrating, but
rather the ability that a child has to receive.

People were bringing little children to Jesus for him to place
his hands on them, but the disciples rebuked them. When

Jesus saw this, he was indignant. He said to them, "Let the little children come to me, and do not hinder them, for the kingdom of God belongs to such as these. Truly I tell you, anyone who will not receive the kingdom of God like a little child will never enter it." And he took the children in his arms, placed his hands on them and blessed them.

I struggled to accept forgiveness when I fell, but children readily accept gifts. Adults struggle and become embarrassed when a gift is given and there is no seasonal excuse for the gift-giving, such as Christmas or a birthday.

Oh, you shouldn't have.

It's too generous.

I didn't get you anything.

I believe that my "adult" intensity was part of my depression. Acknowledging that Jesus knew my fragility and vulnerability, that he wanted me to receive his love and forgiveness simply, like a child, was beyond me then. Surely that would have helped me avoid some of my darker days.

• • •

It's a strange question we British people often ask when we are look-ing for a product to buy. We walk into a store — say, a hardware store — and ask, "I don't suppose you sell screwdrivers, do you?" It's a nonsensical way to carry on, really. If we suspect that they don't carry the product, why on earth are we wasting our time — and theirs — by going in to ask?

But Jesus did just that. His question had a negative expectation built into it: "Haven't you any fish?"

The English translation is very good in this instance: he prefaces his question with a word that anticipates a negative answer. There is an inference, an assumption, that they will answer that, no, it's been a bad night. No fish indeed.

The negative hue of the question seems to diffuse the potential to disappoint; no terrible news needs to be broken; he already suspects that they have had difficulties. It might be that Jesus didn't only know where the fish were, but he knew where the fish were not. Perhaps he just knew his disciples very well, and could probably read the despair on their faces. But the way he puts the question paves the way for them to respond without excuse.

They confess it: their nets are empty. There's no attempt by the disciples to blather on about the ones that got away, the difficult conditions, fish stocks being down, or the fabulous hauls of fish that were normally theirs. They answer with blunt simplicity, without any excuses made.

"No."

They simply own up to the night's failure. He has helped them to do just that and expresses no surprise or disdain.

It might come to us as a surprise that Jesus is never surprised by us. If he is all that he says he is, then he knows every detail of who we are. No hair on our head is uncounted. He does not love us with ridiculously high hopes, nor with a romantic love that screens out our ugliness. A. W. Tozer writes the following:

> How unutterably sweet is the knowledge that our Heavenly Father knows us completely. No talebearer can inform on us, no enemy can make an accusation stick; no forgotten skeleton can come tumbling out of the closest to abash us and expose our past; no unsuspected weakness in our characters can come to light to turn God away from us, since He knew us utterly before we knew Him and called us to Himself in the full knowledge of everything that was against us.

He knows us utterly, and loves us utterly, even when we come to him empty-handed. That's how we were when we first decided to follow him. And that's how those disciples had first met him too, three years earlier. Empty-handed.

Or, more specifically, empty-netted.

• • •

It's called déjà vu. It's that strange nudge where we feel that an episode of our lives is a rerun of something that happened earlier—that we've been here before.

As Jesus offered some specific casting hints to his exhausted friends, Peter, James, and John surely recalled another life-changing day. Three years earlier, when Peter first met Jesus, the adventure had begun with another epic catch, the event that had prompted the fishermen to abandon their trade and begin following Jesus. Luke writes:

> Once when he was standing on the shore of Lake Gennesaret, the crowd was pushing in on him to better hear the Word of God. He noticed two boats tied up. The fishermen had just left them and were out scrubbing their nets. He climbed into the boat that was Simon's and asked him to put out a little from the shore. Sitting there, using the boat for a pulpit, he taught the crowd. When he finished teaching, he said to Simon, "Push out into deep water and let your nets out for a catch."
>
> Simon said, "Master, we've been fishing hard all night and haven't caught even a minnow. But if you say so, I'll let out the nets." It was no sooner said than done—a huge haul of fish, straining the nets past capacity. They waved to their partners in the other boat to come help them. They filled both boats, nearly swamping them with the catch.
>
> Simon Peter, when he saw it, fell to his knees before Jesus. "Master, leave. I'm a sinner and can't handle this holiness. Leave me to myself." When they pulled in that catch of fish,

awe overwhelmed Simon and everyone with him. It was the
same with James and John, Zebedee's sons, coworkers with
Simon.

Jesus said to Simon, "There is nothing to fear. From now on
you'll be fishing for men and women." They pulled their boats
up on the beach, left them, nets and all, and followed him.

It had happened there, on the Sea of Galilee, or Lake Gennesaret
as it's also called. Then, as now, they had spent a whole night working
but had nothing in their nets to show for it. So his command to put
the nets back in was strange. Naturally, those fishermen knew very
well that the best fishing was done by night in the deep water; any
daytime fishing was done in the shallows. But they had obeyed anyway, an impressive act of obedience that would have meant recasting
about a thousand pounds of waterlogged, cumbersome netting. As
they did, that same net began to rip apart under the strain; they were
unable to haul the net onto the boat, so swollen was it with fish.

Fast forward three years, as the stranger tells them where to fish.
The disciples are living a "Groundhog Day," where they find themselves living in a scene that they've lived in before, perhaps to spark
their memories. Perhaps Jesus was enabling his friends to relive a
moment, to nudge them to remember why and how they'd signed
up for this wonderful, bewildering adventure in the first place. But
specifically, that first day of calling had been about their lack, and the
plentiful catch that came from following Jesus' directions.

For Peter, it evoked the memory of how he had felt back then:
unworthy, unclean, and so desperately grimy that he had begged
Jesus to go away. But instead of being rejected, he'd been commis-
sioned to become part of the team.

Perhaps that's part of the purpose of that long night three years
later: these disciples who had all ran when he needed them—including
headstrong Peter, who had denied Christ three times, even though he'd

pledged faithfulness—they all needed to know that they could come to him with a net full of nothing, an offering of failure.

Let's not fool ourselves into believing that we are smiled upon and useful because we are impressive. Perhaps we need to go back to the beginning, to the basics of the gospel. Because we often begin with grace and then feel that we are kept by our works.

But those who trudge home with armfuls of nothing are still welcome to sit down with Jesus.

• • •

Did that huge shoal of fish mysteriously gather in a moment at his command, summoned from the murky depths at his whisper? The rabbis taught that God has authority over fish; perhaps that's the miracle—that they shot to that precise spot at his beckoning.

Or maybe this miracle took another form.

Perhaps the fish had been there all the time, a huge school of them, and the miracle is that the beach-bound Jesus, a hundred yards away, knew exactly where they were to be found. If that's true, it means that the disciples were precisely one boat's width away from a massive catch; they were on the brink of the haul of their lives and on the edge of giving up too.

We quit, not realizing how near we are to success. Sometimes we just need to keep going, regardless. As Woody Allen said, "Ninety percent of success is just showing up." And as we show up, teach that class, care for that unlovely and perhaps ungrateful person, give, serve, hope, and refuse disappointment, then who knows? The answer to that prayer might come tomorrow; the needed breakthrough that we have been desperately looking for might be closer than we think. The disciples would have beached their boat without a catch but for that one last casting.

Being a Christian involves endurance.

Obeying when it's the last thing you want to do.

Getting up and trying again.

Hanging in there.

And so Peter and his friends did as they were told and recast the net. Did it take a few seconds or a minute or two? Suddenly the ropes jerked taut, and then exhausted fishermen scrambled into action. They had a catch, probably the biggest catch of their lives. They hauled in what some interpreters have suggested would have been over three hundred pounds of fish.

• • •

It seems that whenever Jesus took responsibility for the catering arrangements, food and drink were provided in massive quantities. There was the time when five thousand men (plus women and children) were fed, and there were twelve baskets left over. This was not a rationed snack, but a more-than-enough feast, plenty for all and more besides. And when Jesus' ministry was launched at the wedding of Cana (reluctantly, because his mother nudged him into action when the wine ran dry), he didn't just produce a bottle or two, but at least 120 gallons of wonderful wine that tasted like a fine vintage, even though seconds earlier it had been just water.

Now, as the net was just too heavy to haul aboard their boat, teeming with so many fish, once again the catch that Jesus provided was way more than a handful of hungry men could eat for breakfast.

So why is everything "supersized" in these miracles? Surely these are signs that point to God's incredible generosity in the face of our emptiness and comparative poverty. There's nothing meager about him. Paul paints him as being able beyond our capacity to imagine:

And I ask him that with both feet planted firmly on love, you'll be able to take in with all followers of Jesus the extravagant dimensions of Christ's love. Reach out and experience the breadth! Test its length! Plumb the depths! Rise to the heights! Live full lives, full in the fullness of God. God can do anything, you know—far more than you could ever imagine or guess or request in your wildest dreams!

Sometimes I shrink God down to the manageable size of my small hopes, but he was, and is, so much more extravagant. The bulging net speaks of God's huge heart and of blessing his failed friends. And perhaps the bumper catch paved the way to enable Peter to respond rather differently from the way he had acted when he'd first met Jesus.

Back then, three years earlier, he had wanted to run away from Jesus, because of his sin. Now he would run to Jesus, with all his sin, his failure, and his shame. He would run even though it meant leaping out of a boat and wading through chilly water.

But first, of course, someone had to recognize just who the stranger on the shore actually was.

• • •

It was John who finally figured it out. He was usually the first to catch on. The gospels tell us this about John and Peter: Peter always takes action before John, and John always understands before Peter.

Remember resurrection day?

Dashing to the empty tomb, John arrived slightly ahead of Peter—but typical of John, he didn't go right on in, but waited. Peter arrived and marched right into the gloom. Then John follows—and it's John who sees and understands.

Back in the boat, it's John who realizes who their visitor is. He's excited and yells out that, once again, Jesus has come for a meeting. In typical fashion, Peter forgets their awesome catch of fish still flapping around, weighing his boat down, and jumps into the water.

Who knows why he puts his cloak on first? Dressing before swimming seems a little strange. Some say he was half-naked for the fishing work, fine for the boat, inappropriate for the beach. Perhaps his reaching for the cloak was an outward expression of an inner desire: to cover himself up, to hide his shame.

But look at these two in the boat: the thinker and the action man. They discovered Jesus together. They needed each other.

Earlier I talked about becoming prematurely adult. Adults stand on their own two feet. Self-sufficiency is a sign of being very grown up; in this story, however, Peter needed John at his side to enable him to know where Jesus was — hardly self-sufficient or independent.

In my early years, we sang a little song that was effectively a declaration of independence from other human beings:

> *He is all I need*
> *He is all I need*
> *Jesus is all I need.*

I've stopped singing it.

Jesus is not all I need.

He's designed me to need more than him. I'm made to belong, created for friendship by the Trinity that is, mysteriously, a divine company.

The apostle Paul wouldn't sing that song. Instead, he celebrates the function and fellowship of the body of Christ by emphasizing our need of one another:

> For no matter how significant you are, it is only because of what you are a part of. An enormous eye or a gigantic hand wouldn't be a body, but a monster. What we have is one body with many parts, each its proper size and in its proper place. No part is important on its own. Can you imagine Eye telling Hand, "Get lost; I don't need you"? Or, Head telling Foot, "You're fired; your job has been phased out"? As a matter of fact, in practice it works the other way — the "lower"

the part, the more basic, and therefore necessary. You can live without an eye, for instance, but not without a stomach. When it's a part of your own body you are concerned with, it makes *no* difference whether the part is visible or clothed, higher or lower. You give it dignity and honor just as it is, without comparisons. If anything, you have more concern for the lower parts than the higher. If you had to choose, wouldn't you prefer good digestion to full-bodied hair?

The way God designed our bodies is a model for understanding our lives together as a church: every part dependent on every other part, the parts we mention and the parts we don't, the parts we see and the parts we don't. If one part hurts, every other part is involved in the hurt, and in the healing. If one part flourishes, every other part enters into the exuberance. You are Christ's body—that's who you are! You must never forget this. Only as you accept your part of that body does your "part" mean anything.

Jesus wouldn't have joined in with the song we used to sing either. Far from not needing anyone other than his Father, Jesus needed Peter, James, and John as he stood just hours away from trial by a kangaroo court, a near-lynching by Roman thugs, and then execution using one of the most painful methods invented.

Then Jesus went with them to a garden called Gethsemane and told his disciples, "Stay here while I go over there and pray." Taking along Peter and the two sons of Zebedee, he plunged into an agonizing sorrow. Then he said, "This sorrow is crushing my life out. Stay here and keep vigil with me." Going a little ahead, he fell on his face, praying, "My Father, if there is any way, get me out of this. But please, not what I want. You, what do *you* want?" When he came

back to his disciples, he found them sound asleep. He said to
Peter, "Can't you stick it out with me a single hour?"

I didn't realize that my friends help me discover Jesus. Assuming
that solo spirituality was best, and stifled by the false notion that, as a
pastor, I couldn't have friends from among the congregation, I made
the assumption that I had to stand alone.

I've since changed my tune and have heavily invested in a few
very close friendships. When the fog comes and believing seems
absurd, friends can help remind me that Jesus is indeed alive and even
point me in his direction. The picture of Peter and John together is a
living portrait of that truth. But ironically, in a world dominated by
"social" media, building substantial friendships demands intentional-
ity, sacrifice, and ongoing effort.

While most of us have daily contact with many people, our gen-
eration is nevertheless a lonely crowd. In his classic *Bowling Alone*,
sociologist Robert Putman suggests that America's stock of "social
capital"—networks among individuals and the reciprocity and trust-
worthiness that arise from them—has declined substantially over the
past few decades. We are less likely to vote, give blood, play cards,
join in league bowling, or have friends or neighbors over for dinner.
Perhaps some of these opportunities to build social networks have
been replaced with others, such as soccer games or Facebook. Yet we
are increasingly disconnected from family, neighbors, and friends.

The different gifts and character of these two disciples—coming
together—speak to us as well. John was the pondering thinker, Peter
the man of action—but both were vital in their different ways.

I was a pastor. Ministers have to multitask as administrators,
public speakers, scholars, counselors, public servants, as well as be
gifted with enviable HR skills, seeing as they have to manage a workforce of volunteers who can't be disciplined with a pay cut or fired.

I had to function—or at least appear to function—in an array of different skills. When I knew I was being called to function in a sphere that was way out of my gifting, my response was to try to do what seemed beyond me. I didn't know the blessing of realizing my limits and boundaries; I assumed I had to be good at everything, which created more stress.

The Christian subculture is quick to use expansionist language; we're constantly exhorting each other to stretch, take risks, grow, and go out on a limb. "I can't" is not a phrase that Christians generally like. When we insist that we cannot fulfill a function because we are not gifted at it, there's a scriptural phrase that is usually tossed around, in a way that would make the apostle Paul, who first coined it, wince: "I can do all things through Christ who strengthens me." The implication is that we can do anything. But hear this:

We can't.

That's not what Paul meant. He was declaring that whatever he was called by God to do, he would be strengthened for. I can't do everything, even with Jesus in my life. I can't play the bassoon, dance the lead role in *The Nutcracker*, yodel in Spanish, or give birth to twins. I can't do everything, by design.

But back then, I tried. I didn't know how to say no. I thought that faith only enabled me to say what I was good at, and not identify what was actually beyond me. And so I marched resolutely on toward near burnout.

But as Peter and John came together in their differences, the fog cleared. John realized who it was and exclaimed, "It is the Lord." Peter, man of action, needed nothing more. He was a man overboard.

Much of the time I too was a man overboard, but in a different way. I was a man overwhelmed because I didn't know how to say no.

• • •

There's a further detail we could easily miss regarding how the disciples came together. The breakfast could easily have been ruined by a fight breaking out among them, or at least some harsh words spoken and hurt feelings as a result.

As Peter abandons ship and rushes off to see Jesus, think about the other six, left behind to do the hard work of towing the bulging net and then steering the boat to shore. Sure, Peter took it upon himself to complete the final part of the job by jumping into the beached boat and dragging the net ashore. Maybe he was just being helpful, remembering to play his part; this was his boat, after all. But perhaps there was the potential for the others to become irritated with him; they had done the hard work of dragging this ton of fish to shore—and now Peter grabbed the moment and the glory when that work was done, and presented some of the catch to Jesus.

But if there was any irritation (and I'm obviously speculating), no one complained. This team, which had once been threatened by pettiness and competitiveness, had learned some lessons along the way. Jesus had taught them to act like servants, to put each other first. My friend Dary Northrop strips away any romantic notions about our aspiring to be servantlike: "The only way to discover if you're a servant is to see how you act when people treat you like one."

The six steered the boat home with no murmuring recorded. Perhaps it didn't happen that way, and there was no tension in the air.

But if it did, we've just witnessed another quiet miracle.

* * *

Back in the boat, John watched Peter wading through the waves. He's viewing everything with an eagle eye, for he's the reporter who would later chronicle the details of this day.

But he doesn't name himself in his account; he just uses the phrase "the disciple whom Jesus loved." In his letters, he remains unnamed too. In his gospel, he tags himself like that three times—twice in this episode alone. At first glance, it seems arrogant, pretentious even, as if John was striding around flouting this news: Jesus loved me the best.

But look again. It might be the precise opposite.

John never singled himself out to be more loved than anyone else; he simply celebrates the truth that Jesus really did love him so very much. Perhaps preferring the humility of anonymity, John's motive was this: My name is not important. What my parents called me is not the vital issue. What really matters is that I am loved by Jesus.

This truth is so basic to our faith, a truth that at times seems so unfathomable, so vital, that it could have settled my young, enthusiastic heart.

We are loved.

When we bring our offerings of nothing, when our efforts lead to futility, and when believing seems ridiculous, then this remains truer than the names we bear.

We are loved.

5

···

BY THE FIRE

When they landed, they saw a fire of burning coals there with fish on it, and some bread.

Jesus said to them, "Bring some of the fish you have just caught." So Simon Peter climbed back into the boat and dragged the net ashore.

JOHN 21:9 – 11

Christianity, from Golgotha onwards, has been the sanctification of failure.

MALCOLM MUGGERIDGE

Most Christians have enough religion to feel guilty about their sins, but not enough to enjoy life in the spirit.

MARTIN LUTHER

He saw with eyes that saw everything ... all my concealed disgrace and ugliness.... He crawled into my dirtiest nooks. This most curious one had to die.

FRIEDRICH NIETZSCHE

A beach fire is a welcome sight. The warmth of it beckoned the weary but exhilarated disciples, the smell of the broiled fish wafting across the beach. As they landed their boat at last, they realized that Jesus had been busy while waiting for them: breakfast was almost ready. Food always tastes better when shared in the open air, and it was just what they needed for their growling stomachs.

But look again at that fire. Peter certainly did.

Just days earlier Peter had denied that he even knew Jesus. Having vehemently disassociated himself from his friend and rabbi, weighting his words with curses, perhaps he was shocked at himself, stunned because he had crumbled so quickly.

He hadn't endured a terrible beating, the Roman *verberatio*, a horrifying ordeal where the prisoner was scourged with whips made with small pieces of metal or bone, which would literally rip the person apart, often causing death. It didn't take that to melt Peter's resolve.

Maybe his fear and his instinct for survival, stirred by the awful sounds he would have heard from within the high priest's house, overrode his loyalty. Peter would have overheard the terrible sound of knuckles pummeling soft, yielding flesh; the mocking jeers: "Prophesy! Who hit you?"; the solid slaps and the gravelly sound of their throats as they hacked up and festooned him with spit. Peter had tried to be so brave back in Gethsemane, drawing a sword. This was the work of an impetuous but brave heart; he famously denied, but let's never forget that he was the only disciple brave enough to follow the contingent to outside the high priest's home, a dangerous undertaking. He was trying to get close to Jesus in his time of need—to demonstrate that he was in fact loyal to him. But the adrenaline-powered courage that made him a warrior in that moment had deserted him.

Now, warming his hands by a brazier in the courtyard, the flames lit up his face. His heart raced as he noticed that a servant girl standing there was staring at him, realization dawning on her face. She points an accusatory finger and blurts out words that fill him with terror as she makes her indictment:

"This man was with him."

He's quick to try to shut her down, silence her speculations.

"Woman, I don't know him!"

He rubbed his hands again against the cold and stared woodenly ahead, hoping that they wouldn't see the fear in his eyes.

But suspicion had been aroused. Others chimed in.

First they muttered behind cupped hands, glancing his way; then some of the high priest's officials and servants asked him outright. This time he was more emphatic, faking indignation, his voice loud with feigned outrage. Finally a relative of the man who'd had his ear sliced off by Peter in the garden pressed him. In his account of Peter's worst hour, John is at pains to let us know a vital detail: his betrayal took place at a fireside. Following the first denial: "It was cold, and the servants and officials stood around a fire they had made to keep warm. Peter also was standing with them, warming himself."

And then John points out the second time that Peter insisted that Jesus was no friend of his: "Meanwhile, Simon Peter was still standing there warming himself. So they asked him, 'You aren't one of his disciples too, are you?' He denied it, saying, 'I am not.'"

And now, days later, Peter runs up onto the beach—and there's another fire.

Peter looks down with amazement, not at his own hands as he had warmed himself that terrible night, but at the hands of a man who is busily preparing breakfast. These hands are like no other.

Hands like these usually belonged to the dead. Bloodied, bruised. They had holes in them.

Is Jesus taunting Peter, dragging him over the coals, so to speak?

I don't believe so, although Peter might well have been shocked to see that fire. The fire was a reminder of Peter's failure, but surely it was built to bring healing, not torment, because God's grace and forgiveness faces the facts.

God's forgiveness is not about airbrushing out the negative episodes in our histories; rather, it is about actual, real grace that meets actual, real events that we regret.

• • •

The gathered coals of the fire silently said this, loud and clear: the denials happened.

In forgiving us, God makes no attempt to minimize, excuse, or overlook our sins. Peter's failure was not brushed aside or deemed unimportant. We saw earlier that if there was any specific conversation about Peter's denials, it's not recorded; it might have happened two weeks earlier on Easter Day, during that deeply private one-on-one meeting between Jesus and Peter. Perhaps there was no discussion at all, because Jesus is more interested in what causes us to sin rather than the specific action itself. We may be obsessed with behavior, but he wants to go to the heart.

But the fire shows us that in forgiving, Jesus looks squarely at our sin, names it for what it is, and then forgives. His view of our sin is not blinkered or blurred. Just as the crucified Christ looked at his tormenters and cried out to his Father for their forgiveness, so Jesus looks at the ugliness of our darkest sins and then chooses to pardon us, not with a grace that is forgetful, because our sin slips his mind, but rather because he chooses to remember our sins no more. The fire testifies that our sin is real—but the Jesus who sits at the fireside is just as real, and his verdict is trustworthy.

We are forgiven—and this forgiveness is offered to us as we are, not to us as we would like to be.

When Peter had insisted that he alone would be faithful to Jesus, even if everyone else would flee, he was being more than a thoughtless motormouth. I think he was totally sincere in his pledge, which he partly delivered on, misguidedly, when he drew a sword in the garden. His denial in the courtyard meant that he couldn't sustain faithfulness—but when he made his vow, he truly believed that he had what it took. Like all of us, he lacked self-awareness and was blinded to his own limitations. Peter stands alongside the brilliant scholar Augustine: "I had placed myself behind my own back, refusing to see myself."

Donald McCullough, the distinguished college professor I mentioned earlier, speaks movingly of his need to face the truth about himself following his moral failure, divorce, and dismissal from ministry:

My preferred method of dealing with ugliness has been to deny it. I have known it exists, theoretically speaking, and I can certainly spot it in other people. But I have not wanted to accept it as a possibility for me. I have seen myself as different, the exception to the rule. Failure is a reality, to be sure, but I have always had confidence in my ability to get over or around or through it; I have always, up to now, seen my life on an upward trajectory, moving steadily toward the achievement of my dreams.... We are skilled practitioners of the art of selective perception, repressing our fear and guilt and shame into the dark cellars of the unconscious. Running from darkness does not mean running into light. The more we run from it, through denial or willful ignorance, the more its power grows.... We must enter the darkness, not be afraid to stay in it, and then—only then—will the light of knowledge have the chance to illuminate it.

As he felt the warmth of those flames, Peter had to learn that recovery from failure involves not only facing it, his sin, but facing himself, the sinner. Take grace out of the equation, and we might be tempted to hopelessness. But grace welcomes Peter, not the faithful, saintly, strong version of Peter that he wanted to be, but the fickle, cussing, temperamental, impulsive, and weak man that Peter was.

And so it is with us.

• • •

This was a juncture moment for Peter because, as we'll see, he would be invited to offer words of fresh loyalty and love for Jesus, following a time of silence and then breakfast at the fireside. Shame has the capacity to silence our worship; just as we come to lift up our hearts and hands, we realize again that they are far from holy, and we back away, confused, bewildered. Overwhelming shame renders us speechless.

But Jesus located himself in Peter's story and, more importantly, helped Peter to relocate himself once again in God's story, helping him to realize that even his sin could not cancel out the love Jesus had for him or nullify the love that Peter had for Christ. By our own firesides we offer our love to God and come to find out that we will not be rejected or scorned.

How I struggled to accept forgiveness. I believed in it theologically but could not accept it emotionally. Little wonder I felt so depressed. Of course, I was not alone.

David Seamands, a counselor, reports that even if we say that grace is amazing, many of us don't accept it for our specific failures:

We read, we hear, we believe a good theology of grace. But that's not the way we live. We believe grace in our heads but not in our gut feelings.... There's no other word we throw around so piously. We affirm grace in our creeds and sing about it in our hymns. We proclaim it as distinctive of the Christian faith—that we are saved by grace alone through faith. But it's all on a head level. The good news of the Gospel of grace has not penetrated the level of our emotions.

We are called to worship as the forgiven ones, not despite what happened by the fireside of our failures, but because of God's response to what did happen there. Peter had to face the fire, but it was not fiery judgment. Still, he struggled to accept that forgiveness.

• • •

Washing sweaty, dusty feet isn't a high priority on most people's agendas. Not only was it a deeply unpleasant task, but it carried a stigma with it; not even Jewish slaves were required to pick up the towel and the bowl. It was a job usually reserved for those at the bottom of the social food chain.

That's why the disciples were so stunned to see Jesus, their esteemed rabbi, take the job on. They'd probably felt it would have been beneath them to pick up the bowl and towel themselves—nobody would ever wash the feet of their peers—but now he took the initiative.

Slowly he did the grubby work, and quietly, perhaps with some embarrassment, the disciples let him do it. Even Judas, betrayal already in his heart, submitted himself to the cleansing ritual. But there was one who protested, whose outburst halted the washing.

That would be Peter.

Jesus knew that the Father had put all things under his power, and that he had come from God and was returning to God; so he got up from the meal, took off his outer clothing, and wrapped a towel around his waist. After that, he poured water into a basin and began to wash his disciples' feet, drying them with the towel that was wrapped around him.

He came to Simon Peter, who said to him, "Lord, are you
going to wash my feet?"

Jesus replied, "You do not realize now what I am doing,
but later you will understand."

"No," said Peter, "you shall never wash my feet."

Jesus answered, "Unless I wash you, you have no part with
me."

"Then, Lord," Simon Peter replied, "not just my feet but
my hands and my head as well!"

Peter wanted to serve Jesus but couldn't cope with the idea of
Jesus serving him like a slave. He was learning that the only way to
be around Jesus was allowing him to clean you up. This was not a
luxurious option. It was the only way. Peter could have no part with
Jesus unless he submitted himself to this arrangement:

You bring your emptiness. He fills you.

You bring your grime. He washes you.

A sense of helplessness and humility of heart is needed if we're to
do absolutely nothing other than receive.

I'll put it starkly.

Jesus comes to be our slave as well as our savior. He is the suffering servant not only of his father, but of us all. He humbles himself
and yet, ironically, calls us to acknowledge our utter helplessness and
humility as he kneels before us with the bowl and towel.

Like Peter, I struggled with such scandalous, free forgiveness. I
wrestled with God.

• • •

Wrestling is a much-loved sport in my family. Back in England in the
mid-1960s, Aunt Hetty, save for earthquake, flood, or apocalypse,
would be found in her usual place each week, ensconced in a plump
couch in front of the television watching the Saturday afternoon

wrestling. Rotund chaps with exotic names such as Big Daddy, Jackie Pallo, and Mick McManus, some of whom apparently trained by eating way too many cheeseburgers, would whip the blood hungry crowd into a frenzy. They would then grapple and grunt and tumble and twist their way to victory.

Some were quite literally larger than life, such as the Goliath-like Giant Haystacks, which I suspect was not actually the name his mother gave him. Just an inch under seven feet tall, this bearded behemoth weighed in at no less than 670 pounds. The classic bad guy who everyone loved to hate, Giant Haystacks was actually a devout Christian who refused to wrestle on Sundays. Perhaps they called him Brother Haystacks in his church.

No matter that the wrestling was rather obviously choreo-graphed; Britain lapped it up. A considerable lady, Aunt Hetty would park herself in front of the black-and-white screen, hugging a cup of hot tea the size of a chamber pot. Beside her sat Uncle John, a diminutive, and therefore nervous, man. Before long, she would start yelling at the screen, and poor Uncle John would tremble, fearing he might end up in a half nelson himself. The aim of the game was to get your rival to submit, which was achieved by tying their limbs up in what looked like a reef knot. Jackie Pallo's party trick was to yell, "Give in, you fool!" at opponents who resisted a submission hold.

Wrestling is an activity found in the big story of Scripture, and throughout history human beings have consistently tried to take on the biggest daddy of them all: God.

Jacob is a famous wrestler who began his career early with an in-womb struggle with his brother Esau. But his most famous bout was with the Lord in an all-nighter when he insisted, "I will not let you go unless you bless me." Their ensuing match led to a thigh strain and a lifelong limp. And throughout her history, Israel resisted, struggled, disobeyed, and fought against the loving purposes of God, causing him to complain, "My people would not listen to me; Israel would not submit to me."

But wrestling didn't just happen because of disobedience. Many times, human beings grappled with God not because he was asking them to do something especially difficult, but because they resisted his wonderful grace; they felt that his news to them was just too good to be true. Moses was called to an astounding destiny and stammered that he wasn't up to the job. Trembling Gideon was told he was a mighty warrior, and a protracted argument began. Most of our fights are with God's scandalous forgiveness. We argue and struggle, wanting to pay, like the protesting prodigal squirming in his father's embrace. Ironically, when we resist God's forgiveness, we insist that our authority is higher than his.

We claim that we're not worthy. He says we've been made worthy.

C. S. Lewis calls us away from resisting or wrestling with God, especially when he comes with grace and good news: "I think that if God forgives us we must forgive ourselves. Otherwise it is almost like setting up ourselves as a higher tribunal than Him."

I spent a lot of time wrestling, which meant that the good news became less than good. And when we live like that, we turn Jacob's plea inside out, and cry, "I will not let you bless me—let me go."

I needed to hear Mr. Jackie Pallo's words and yield to the outrageous grace of God, for peace can come when we surrender to love: Give in, you fool.

But sometimes that's easier said—and believed—than done. It's such a big challenge, I wrote a book specifically about it, called *Walking Backwards*. Allow me to share a few observations from it

• • •

Perhaps these words are familiar:

> *There is a fountain filled with blood*
> *Drawn from Emmanuel's veins;*

And sinners plunged beneath that flood
  Lose all their guilty stains. . . .

E'er since by faith, I saw the stream
  Thy flowing wounds supply,
Redeeming love has been my theme,
  And shall be till I die.

They were penned by William Cowper, one of the greatest poets
and hymn writers of the eighteenth century. But Cowper, cursed
with a weak conscience, never felt he had lost all his own guilty
stains. Wracked by terrible periods of depression that drove him to
attempt suicide, he was convinced that he could never be forgiven
for his own iniquities, and called himself "damned beyond Judas."
Even Cowper's close friend John Newton, writer of "Amazing Grace,"
was unable to assure him that he was saved. As a result, he did not
die with love as his recurring theme; he died believing that he was
beyond forgiveness.

Tragically, many of us live that way. We name ourselves after our
greatest failure. Michelangelo Buonarroti (1475–1564) was one of
the greatest artists of all time, a man whose name has become syn-
onymous with the word masterpiece. As an artist he was unmatched,
creating works of sublime beauty that express the full breadth of the
human condition.

But he was a socially inept, insecure man — the enmity between
him and Leonardo da Vinci is famous. He had episodes of crippling
self-doubt and crises of confidence in his own ability. During the
painting of *Creation Day* on the ceiling of the Sistine Chapel, he had
a particularly difficult day up on the backbreaking scaffolding. That
night, the great man wrote these words in his journal: "I am not a
painter."

How often are we temporarily blinded to our own abilities? How
often do we lie about ourselves and therefore rush to conclude that

we are liars. Our addiction to shame numbs our awareness of any goodness within us.

John Quincy Adams was convinced that his life was pretty much a waste of time: "My life has been spent in vain and idle aspirations, and in ceaseless rejected prayers that something beneficial should be the result of my existence."

Adams felt that he had accomplished nothing, even though he had served as the American ambassador to Holland, Great Britain, and Russia, as well as secretary of state, senator, and ultimately, president of the United States.

Shame is a powerfully blinding force.

• • •

One of my challenges in my perception of myself was that I had a simplistic view of my emotional makeup, which, of course, is anything but simple. If I felt guilty, I just assumed that God's Holy Spirit was convicting me. It didn't occur to me that my obsessive personality might be working overtime or that my negative caricatures of God made it difficult for me to enjoy anything that was too much fun or pleasurable; I interpreted every twinge of conscience as a message from heaven.

Quack theology made me sicker.

Someone ventured that because the Bible teaches that we should always let our conscience be our guide, then my negative feelings were most likely messengers from God. I searched high and low for that Scripture about our conscience being our guide. I pored over a huge concordance for ages—this was the world before Google—to try to pin it down. Was it in the gospels, or Proverbs perhaps, or maybe one of Paul's letters?

Finally I found it.

This wisdom came not from Scripture, but from the story of Pinocchio. The wooden chap was obviously a great sinner—that's how he got his telescopic nose. But thankfully, he was rescued from his deceptive ways by a little green insect with a moral heart and a catchy tune: Jiminy Cricket.

Of course, the conscience is a vital element to our moral compass, but it's not infallible. J. B. Phillips warns:

> To make conscience into God is a highly dangerous thing to do. For one thing ... conscience is by no means an infallible guide; and for another it is extremely unlikely that we shall ever be moved to worship, love, and serve a nagging inner voice that at worst spoils our pleasure and at best keeps us rather negatively on the path of virtue. Conscience can be so easily perverted or morbidly developed in the sensitive person, and so easily ignored and silenced by the insensitive, that it makes a very unsatisfactory God. For while it is probably true that every normal person has an embryo moral sense by which he can distinguish right and wrong, the development, non-development, or perversion of that sense is largely a question of upbringing, training and propaganda.

I had an overactive conscience; I was one of what the Catholics call the "scrupulous." No matter how hard I tried, I never felt a sense of arrival or accomplishment. What I did was never enough. I walked a kind of treadmill, but there was no power button to switch the ever-turning belt off. I constantly questioned and monitored myself, wondering if I was truly useful.

Do some of our church services, with their weekly calls to do better, work harder, and get more holy, actually torment the scrupulous? Are our gatherings laced with grace — or relentless guilt? Because they feel worthless, the permanently guilty are usually busy people, taking a pack-mule approach to life. Perhaps if they can just work harder, they can prove themselves worthy. The guilty soul seldom says no to yet more work—the beast of burden gets more and more exhausted.

Typically, compulsive shame and a damaged conscience can result from being raised on a constant emotional diet of being told that we are no good.

That message is difficult to undo.

Shame addicts are also created by churches that are more "guilt machines" than communities of grace. The church where I began the Christian life was the opposite—a warm, human place to be—but some churches are comprised of people who assemble weekly to collectively feel bad together. One gets the impression that the only way to come to God is with tears and remorse. Fun is suspect.

We can also slide into shame addiction when we have been guilty of spectacular, lurid sin, and we have repented but can't forgive ourselves or accept that we have been forgiven. This is especially true with sexual sin, which has a tendency to shame us more than failure in other areas. The greater the potential for embarrassment, the higher the capacity for shame.

Peter sat in silence by a fire because he needed to know that forgiveness was specific, solid, and reliable. He had to trust God's verdict, whatever his shameful feelings.

Sadly, some of us have a faith that is dominated by subjective feelings. Christians often talk about "feeling" forgiven, as if an elusive feeling is the final stamp of confirmation that grace is truly ours.

But our feelings lie. We feel defeated, our heads bowed, our hearts heavy. Sometimes the cost of unresolved shame is higher.

Sometimes it's a matter of life and death.

In my book *Grace Choices*, I shared a tragic story that has left a permanent mark on my life:

John—not his real name—was a bright, popular guy who seemed to enjoy his work as an associate pastor in the church across town in the English Midlands. I never knew him that well, but he seemed to be intelligent and confident, enjoying life. But his smile masked an inner darkness. Prior to entering full time ministry, John had lived for a year or two in open rebellion towards God. He wasn't just immoral—he was perversely immoral in his passion for sexual deviancy. Then John came back to God. His repentance was total, his commitment unquestioned. But the sickening images of his past stained his soul. Try as he might, he couldn't forget the evil in his personal history. He became convinced that he had blasphemed the Holy Spirit, that he had bypassed the possibility of forgiveness, even though his life and conduct clearly showed that the Holy Spirit was working overtime in his life and had been for years. My telephone screamed at 3:00 a.m. It was John's minister. John had disappeared, leaving a note on his door: "Burn my clothes, and consign my soul to hell." He read in his Bible that some would be saved, but only by fire. He put his Bible down. He wrote his note. He went out into a lonely, windswept field, poured a can of gasoline over his head and burned himself to death. This was no calm, martyr's death—he breathed his last in agony. Perhaps John stepped over the threshold into mental illness; who knows what drives people when they find themselves in such deep personal despair? But, whatever the final diagnosis, one thing is sure: false guilt was his executioner. False guilt. Not something I should endure, perversely, for his Name's sake. Not just an incidental problem for the spiritually sensitive. False guilt—brutal murderer; John's killer.

Shame is a stealth weapon that quietly devastates and depresses; it is a thief that plunders our joy, a mugger that mounts a surprising assault, leaving us bruised and bewildered. Over breakfast, Jesus gently began to rescue Peter from shame's clutches.

• • •

Forgiveness is not just about receiving; it enables us to give, to participate once again, and know that what we offer will be received with encouragement. Breakfast on the beach was ready. Jesus had already fixed the fish and bread. But rather than telling his friends not to bother with their nets — forget it, I've already got plenty — he invited them to contribute some of the fish they'd just caught to the breakfast feast. It's a treasure that's crammed into just one word: you.

Bring some of the fish that *you've* just caught.

Stop right there. Those seasoned fishermen had worked long hours through the night, with nothing to show for it. It was only when Jesus stepped in with supernatural net-casting directions (more accurate than any modern fish finder) that anything was caught at all. This was Jesus' catch; theirs was just the small contribution of casting the net and pulling it back in. He could have pointed out that it was only with his help that a big breakfast was possible.

But instead he designates the catch as theirs.

What stunning generosity, and how often he does this! We achieve what we do because of gifts that he gives and opportunities that he opens for us. Good things happen because he empowers us, directs us, and sustains us.

Without him, we can do nothing. Left to our own devices, the nets will always come up empty. But then, at the end of all things, he'll give the rewards to us, as if the achievements along the way were ours.

Our catch.

I have been in church services where dignity was a casualty. I couldn't fault the words being used: we are sinners, and sometimes we do need a wake-up call to stir us from complacency. Unfortunately, I've seen people hollered at, threatened, and then herded around like cattle.

Ironically, not only is this an assault on self-respect, I suspect it doesn't produce lasting fruit anyway. When human beings believe that they are trash, they tend to act like trash. And worse, it gives an impression that God loves to trample our dignity, humiliate, and belittle us.

The real Jesus, however, invites us to bring some of his fish to the table.

And he calls it our fish.

• • •

The fire was obviously built to facilitate a meal: fish on hot coals, and some bread. Whether it was intentional or not, the fact that Jesus was sharing a meal, especially with Peter, spoke volumes about acceptance and grace. It's been said that Jesus was not crucified primarily because of his teaching, but rather his eating habits. For us, a shared meal is a relatively neutral act: we just happen to be eating together, end of story.

But in Near Eastern thinking, sharing a meal with another was viewed as an act of intimacy and fellowship — to offer hospitality was to give honor and trusting acceptance. Refusal to share a meal conversely signaled rejection and disapproval. That's one of the reasons why the Pharisees hated Jesus — they were obsessed with the issue of table fellowship. Radicals who wanted God's holiness to be expressed in every area of daily life insisted that each meal be like an act of worship in the temple. They created a labyrinth of rules about eating, with 229 texts of regulations about how a meal should be shared and with whom. Their food, which had to have been subject to tithing, was carefully prepared with ritual hand washings, and one could not share a meal with anyone who might "defile" the proceedings. Some scholars describe them as "a table fellowship sect."

That's why Jesus created such a stir, because not only did he fraternize with the wrong crowd, but by sharing meals with them he was including them. The religious culture of the day, on the other hand, had firmly parked them outside. Jesus welcomed the pariahs of his world as he ate with those who were despised by the respectable.

"All the people saw this and began to mutter, 'He has gone to be the guest of a sinner.'"

"Now the tax collectors and sinners were all gathering around to hear Jesus. But the Pharisees and the teachers of the law muttered, 'This man welcomes sinners and eats with them.'"

This beautiful sentence from the Anglican Communion service captures the heart of those messianic meals: "He touched untouchables with love and washed the guilty clean." And now, failed Peter was invited to sit down and share a meal with Jesus once more.

Another sinner welcomed.

Fast-forward a decade or so from that fireside encounter. Peter is again weary, not because of a long night's failed fishing, but because he simply needed lunch. Falling into a trance as he prayed, he was treated to a strange vision.

He saw heaven opened and something like a large sheet being let down to earth by its four corners. It contained all kinds of four-footed animals, as well as reptiles and birds. Then a voice told him, "Get up, Peter. Kill and eat."

"Surely not, Lord!" Peter replied. "I have never eaten anything impure or unclean."

The voice spoke to him a second time, "Do not call anything impure that God has made clean."

This happened three times, and immediately the sheet was taken back to heaven.

This paved the way for the conversion of the Gentiles. For the first decade of the church's history, it had been a messianic Jewish group, but now, as the despised Gentiles were finding a warm welcome at God's table, Peter had to learn that what God declares to be clean, we should not call unclean. But a decade earlier, by the fire on that beach, Peter had to learn that about his own grimy failures and about himself.

God's verdict was in.

Forgiven.

Cleansed.

Finished.

So don't argue. Don't call unclean what God has called clean.

6

• • •

LET'S EAT

Jesus said to them, "Come and have breakfast." None of the disciples dared ask him, "Who are you?" They knew it was the Lord. Jesus came, took the bread and gave it to them, and did the same with the fish. This was now the third time Jesus appeared to his disciples after he was raised from the dead.

JOHN 21:12 – 14

Your brain is physically injured, and like any other part of the body that has received a physical injury, it needs the proper care to heal … The problem that far too many people have is that they can't see the injury, therefore it is not a real injury …

JEROD POORE

Your mother was right. Breakfast really is the most important meal of the day.

A healthy breakfast kick-starts the metabolism, improves our motor coordination, and enables us to concentrate — it's the fuel we need to replenish the tank. Without it, we can function, but there'll be some juddering, some anxiety, because the needle is moving perilously closer to the E.

First things first.

Jesus invited his friends to eat with him. Before any conversation, recommissioning, or sharing of prophetic words, came his invitation.

Eat.

The cold, tired, hungry disciples were not invited to a prayer meeting or a teaching session, but to a meal. Fish and bread. Often when God's women and men are down and out, bone weary of work, starved of hope, and smothered with despair, the word of the Lord comes to them.

Let's eat.

Many years earlier, terrified Elijah fled from his nemesis, Jezebel, the Old Testament Cruella de Vil. Prophets usually see straight in the future, with 20/20 vision into what is not yet. But depressed prophets don't see anything much at all, in the past, present, or future. The usually courageous Elijah, his bravery derailed by fear, was suffering some of the classic symptoms of clinical depression:

Hopelessness.
An inability to cope.
A sense of being totally overwhelmed.
Utter inadequacy.
Zero energy or motivation.

A desire to do little other than sleep.
Writing off everything that's been achieved as useless.
Fearing the worst.
Disappointment with God, insisting that it's all been a
    waste of time.
Irrational thinking.

Logic is often one of the first casualties when depression descends, and clarity is stifled by the smothering blanket of deep sadness. Elijah ran for his life and then prayed for his death, which doesn't make a lot of sense. But then, depression acts like a narcotic, stupefying the sufferer, conning them with the most outrageous lies about themselves, about others, and about God.

What was God's response to his fugitive prophet? He dispatched an angel, charged with a special mission as a short-order cook.

The angel touched the slumbering Elijah.

Hey. Let's eat.

There's a fire, with fresh bread baked. Some water.

Elijah eats and drinks, then sleeps some more. Later, the tenacious angel comes back again.

Let's eat again.

An explosive, supernatural encounter with God would follow too, but that came after food, drink, and rest. Finally, after a six-week trek through the wilderness, God finally gave Elijah an eye-popping, heart-stirring pyrotechnic display, and recommissioned him. But food and water came first.

Back at the beach, Jesus warmly offered a similar invitation: Come and have breakfast. Let's eat. Jesus didn't immediately zoom in on what we might think of as spiritual issues: faithfulness, calling, guidance for the future. Instead, he focused on their basic physical needs.

Eating is a very human thing to do. Hunger and thirst are the shared experience of every person on earth. When we feel low, we can be quick to hunt for a deep reason for our sadness, and usually it's a hunt for what we've done wrong, how we've sinned, ways we've failed in prayer and in our faith. Depression makes us an ideal landing spot for condemnation. But before we go on that shame safari, we need to give attention to a more obvious checklist:

> Are we eating healthily and regularly?
> Are we making use of the endorphin surges that can lift our
>   hearts after we've exercised?
> Are we overusing alcohol?
> Are we taking time to laugh and cry with trusted friends?
> Are we making time for nonproductive relaxation?

I know, all of these are very basic, human needs. And some of us need to be more at ease with being human. For in our desire to become more spiritual, some seem to want to get away from our humanity. But our created humanity is God's idea, his design, and he originally declared it to be a very good idea indeed.

• • •

Perhaps we misunderstand the New Testament word *flesh*, as if to be a flesh-and-bone human being is a negative thing. But Paul never suggests that there's a problem with being human. Rather, in the New Testament, especially in Paul's epistles, the word *flesh* is used to describe the fallen, sinful, deteriorated human nature.

It seems we are living with a big fat Greek hangover, the notion that anything physical is negative, and that we should focus on the "spiritual." Greek philosophy, with champions like Plato, insisted that a person's body was evil and that only their spirit was good, a view that totally clashes with the Bible's view on the universe, where the physical, tangible world is described as good. But this lingering notion creates a reluctance to talk, especially on Sunday mornings, about anything relating to the physical realm, such as sex, food, and fun. Our Jewish friends take a much more holistic view of life and of God's involvement in everything.

This negative attitude toward our humanness had led to some twisted ideas about Jesus throughout church history. One of the most prevalent of these heresies is Docetism, the notion that Jesus did not really become a real flesh-and-blood human, but that he just appeared to be human. The heresy insists that Jesus' body was either an illusion or a phantasm. It's a heresy that is alive and well today, rearing its head some years ago at a conference I attended.

A fellow speaker suggested that Jesus would have had bowel movements, and thus needed to use the toilet while on this earth, a perfectly normal biological function and a very obvious part of his life as a human being. Some revolted at the idea, suggesting that this was irreverent talk. In a desire to preserve the truth that Jesus is divine, they wanted to distance him from the very mundane, ordinary, and earthy aspects of his being fully human.

I get nervous when I hear preachers say that "Jesus was God with skin on," which is dangerously close to Docetism. Jesus wasn't God disguised. In a way that we can't begin to grasp, he laid aside the attributes of his divinity and came and "moved into the neighborhood," as Eugene Peterson puts it, as a human being. He lived the life of faith in exactly the same way as we do, battling temptation, praying tearful, sometimes desperate prayers, experiencing fatigue, disappointment, and depression. His despair in the garden of Gethsemane, and his extreme physical response—bleeding through his pores as he faced the prospect of interrogation, trial, and torturous execution—shows he was overwhelmed by anguish.

Does all this matter? It matters a great deal.

First off, it affects the way I look at Jesus. If I understand Jesus as only divine but not fully human, then I think of him as a demanding despot who has no understanding of what it is like to live everyday life on earth. But his humanness doesn't just mean that he can identify with us, but also that he is able to empathize with us too, as we face the challenges of doing life as humans.

> For we do not have a high priest who is unable to empathize with our weaknesses, but we have one who has been tempted in every way, just as we are—yet he did not sin. Let us then approach God's throne of grace with confidence, so that we may receive mercy and find grace to help us in our time of need.

The writer to the Hebrews, in calling us to prayer when we're struggling, insists that we know that we'll find a sympathetic and empathic God when we draw near to him by faith. Jesus understands our dark feelings, our doubt, our discouragement, and yes, even our depressions—and his desire is to help us. He knows what it's like to be us.

This is a beautiful truth and a far cry from the Jesus that I tried to follow during my depression, who was the antithesis of empathy; he just demanded more, mocked my weariness, told me to grow up, die to self, and cajoled me for my weakness. Understanding this shapes the way we look at life, keeping us from dangerously dividing it into "spiritual" and "unspiritual" boxes. For a time, I was overwhelmed because I didn't feel I was spending enough time in "spiritual" pursuits; only if I did would I feel approved of by God. That's part of the reason for the hymn-filled honeymoon for my wife and me, which I mentioned earlier.

When we find ourselves battling depression, we can be deluded into thinking that "spiritual" solutions to periods of despair and depression are superior. We might think that if we find relief through prayer ministry, fasting, and reflection, and by immersing ourselves in biblical study, then we are more godly. But if we find help by considering our diet, ensuring that we get enough sleep, exercising, and prioritizing time for fun and friendship—these are inferior, and we have failed on the "spiritual" battlefield, resorting to more "carnal" resources. Even if we feel better, our victory is vaguely tainted.

On the beach, food and friendship were on the menu, as well as prophecy and counsel. As "the good physician," Jesus treated them not as a Greek Gnostic or dualist philosopher would, but as the God who created them to be whole persons. Rather obviously, our bodies affect our brains, and some of us need to recognize that truth, especially when we're encouraged to seek professional help or take medication. That's when some Christians go into guilt overdrive.

Sometimes, when a physician writes out a prescription for anxiety or depression, suddenly other Christians start writing the person off, as if taking medication is a sign of failure. I've met hundreds of Christians who went to their doctor for help because they feel consistently bad, and when they shared with fellow believers that they were taking those tablets, they were made to feel even worse.

The cause of some depression is rooted in brain chemistry. Rather obviously, the brain is an organ that is profoundly affected by chemical changes, surpluses or deficiencies, as well as genetics. Just as a bruise on my arm has nothing to do with my faith, so some depression is not about embracing a bad, negative, or unbelieving attitude, but may be a simple chemical chain reaction. Christians know that their bodies are going to ache, creak, and ultimately wear out. This is not a matter of whether we are Christian or not—it just happens to us humans. Good, faithful Christians are affected by diseases of the brain, such as Alzheimer's or other forms of dementia.

But some enthusiastic Christians will simply not accept that clinical depression might also have specific biological causes. If they break a limb, they are happy to have that limb placed in plaster so that long-term healing might result. But when they have trouble with what is happening in their heads, they feel reluctant and guilty. I've met too many Christians who have shared their struggle with long-term depression in hushed tones, quite smeared by irrational shame.

But depression, according to the World Health Organization, is the second most common cause of disability worldwide after cardio-vascular disease, and it's on the increase. Depression is expected to become the number one disabler in the next ten years, and people of faith are not exempt. On the contrary. The following paragraph contains some statistics, which might tempt some to pass over it, but please don't. It's vital news. Professor Dan Blazer, professor of psychiatry and behavioral sciences at Duke University Medical Center, writes:

> In the United States, 5 to 10 percent of adults currently experience the symptoms of major depression ... and up to 25 percent meet the diagnostic criteria during their lifetime, making it one of the most common conditions treated by primary care physicians. At any given time, around 15 percent of American adults are taking antidepressant medications. Studies of religious groups, from Orthodox Jews to evangelical Christians, reveal no evidence that the frequency of depression varies across religious groups or between those who attend religious services and those who do not. So in a typical congregation of 200 adults, 50 attendees will experience depression at some point, and at least 30 are currently taking antidepressants.

Despite the fact that millions battle emotional darkness, many Christians still compound their struggle with irrational shame when they turn for help. Mark Mounts, a pastor, is one example:

> After weeks of therapy, my therapist told me I was a good candidate for anti-depressant medication. At first I felt like a total failure. Me ... a Christian pastor ... needed ... happy pills!

So my therapist wisely explained to me in understandable terms what was going on biologically in my brain, and how the medications would help. It had nothing to do with demons, not being good enough, or not being converted. I was able to understand that I was one of those people who had a vulnerability to depression. In my case, my therapist had realized that anti-depressant medication was not the first resort. But as he began to understand my situation, he realized medication could help....

So, I decided to take the medication, and what a difference it has made. You have to be aware of something regarding these medications. People are different, and our body chemistries differ greatly. So, be patient! These medications take several weeks to show results, and they may have side effects. Those can eventually go away; they did for me. But if they don't, there are other medications you can try. The key is to find one that works for you and realize it may not be the first one you try; so hang in there!

Anti-depressant medications are not happy pills. They certainly were not for me. But they did lift the cloud so I could begin to talk about how I was thinking and feeling. Before taking the medication, talking about my thoughts or feelings would only add to my depression. The medication changed that. I still had to talk, and I stayed in counseling for more than a year. I learned that I had been taught some pretty unhealthy ways to think about people and situations. But, thanks to a great counselor, a loving and supportive family, anti-depressant medication, and most importantly, a loving and forgiving God, the cloud finally lifted.

If medication is prescribed for us, we should make use of it without guilt or shame. The same minister writes candidly about the times when we need to seek professional help:

With prayer, "all things are possible," but escaping from depression that is due to a chemical imbalance in the body through prayer alone is not probable. Those who try to dissuade religious people from getting medical help for clinical depression, claiming that faith alone is the cure, can do devastating harm. In many cases, a severe depression that lasts more than a few days is bio-physically based and requires medical treatment. This is certainly true for any who suffer from a bipolar condition. A psychiatrist is trained to diagnose both medical and mental causes of depression. To seek such treatment does not denote a lack of faith, but rather evidence of a willingness to take advantage of what God has made available to us through modern science.

We need to take care when making swift generalizations about the causes of depression, which is why I have stated that some depression is chemically rooted. Sweeping statements can reduce people with depression to being ill people with "broken bodies and brains that need fixing," as Dan Blazer puts it, and can ignore other factors.

Some are depressed because they have succumbed to consistently negative thinking patterns, especially in appraising themselves. They feel inferior and powerless. Others battle with loneliness, negative social environments, or apparently insurmountable problems that lead them to lose all hope. Still others battle because of deep trauma from their past, often because they have been sinned against. And some of what we might label depression is not actually depression at all, but a period of emotional blueness that is a perfectly normal part of life.

Just as the healthy body feels pain when exposed to danger (and the loss of that ability to feel creates huge damage, as leprosy sufferers know only too well), so it's healthy to be grieved, distressed, and saddened. Consistent happiness is not only unrealistic in terms of expectations, it's abnormal.

• • •

Look at those disciples again. They're having a tough day. They're following Christ—but their confusion, their futile night's work, their tiredness is affecting them, just as those elements would affect any normal human being. Their faith does not make them impervious to the blues.

As I mentioned, we can rush too quickly to label a period of sadness in a person's life as depression, which might create greater psychological problems. In their book *The Loss of Sadness*, Professors Allan Horwitz and Jerome Wakefield argue that psychiatrists no longer provide room for their clients' sadness or life's usual ups and downs, labeling even normal mood fluctuations "depression."

But we're not promised unending emotional equilibrium, never mind constant happiness. As compassionate people who are called to weep with those who weep, we should be distressed and saddened at the injustices and tragedies that surround us. Just as Jesus wept over Jerusalem because he loved the people of that city, so we will experience times when our hearts are heavy. We've already seen that the disciples had experienced a tremendous amount of grief and stress in recent days—the sadness they were feeling was perfectly normal. Jesus' prophetic insight triggered sadness in him. If we have grown numb to pain and suffering around us, we have lost a key element of our humanity. Endless delight is not a realistic goal for everyday life; normality includes seasons of sadness:

• • •

The "normal" human life isn't what is marketed to us by the pharmaceutical industry or by the lives we see projected on movie screens, or, frankly, by a lot of Christian sermons and

praise songs. The normal human life is the life of Jesus of Nazareth, who sums up in himself everything it means to be human.
And the life of Christ presented to us in the Gospels is a life
of joy, of fellowship, of celebration, but also of loneliness, of
profound sadness, of lament, of grief, of anger, of suffering, all
without sin.

As the Holy Spirit conforms us to the image of Christ, we
don't become giddy, or, much less, emotionally vacant. Instead,
the Bible tells us we "groan" along with the persecuted creation
around us. We cry out with Jesus himself, experiencing with
him often the agony of Gethsemane. And, paradoxically, along
the way, we join Jesus in joy and peace. A human emotional
life is complicated, and a regenerated human emotional life is
complicated too.

The same writer has a realistic view of the benefits — and the
limitations — of medications. His comments offer a useful balance;
medication might be a vital component in helping us climb out of
the slough of depression but shouldn't be viewed as a magic potion
to lighten every load:

There are some Christians who believe any psychiatric drug
is a spiritual rejection of the Bible's authority. I'm not one of
them. But there are other Christians who seem to think, with
the culture around us, that everything is material and can be
solved by material means. I don't think that's right either. Keep
working with your doctors to treat your depression. If you're
not happy with the treatment or with the side-effects, seek
some additional medical opinion, and listen for wisdom in a
multitude of counselors.... Sometimes the side-effects of these
drugs are awful. Communicate with your doctor, and read up
to ask the right kinds of questions. But spend time too with

those who know you and love you, and ask if there's more behind this than simply serotonin reception. God doesn't want
you to be simply, in the words of one observer of the current
pharmacological utopianism, "comfortably numb." He wants
you to be whole.

• • •

Through the disciples' doubts, their confusion, Jesus kept appearing
to them, assuring them and preparing them for what lay ahead. The
breakfast on the beach is a demonstration not only of the power of
Jesus — in the miraculous catch at his word — but also the patience
of Jesus too.

But remarkably, even though they had so many questions, and
now they had an opportunity to put them to Jesus, they ate breakfast
in silence.

Picture them there.

The sea is lapping behind them.

He prods the coals again with a piece of driftwood but still says
nothing. Initially the absence of words creates a sense of tension but
then perhaps settles into the comfortable quiet shared among close
friends who can be together without words.

Silence.

Not even the anticipated chatter that Peter usually produced.

It's a strange, almost bewildering statement: none of the disciples
dared ask him who he was — they knew it was the Lord. Untangle
that one, if you will. They'd been in that place before, where dozens of questions lined up impatiently in their minds, but they were
reluctant to ask any of them. There was that time when they returned
from a shopping trip in town to find him beside a well, chatting
with a woman from Samaria: "Just then his disciples returned and
were surprised to find him talking with a woman. But no one asked,
'What do you want?' or 'Why are you talking with her?'"

I tend to be full of questions, and I'm convinced that questioning is a great way to grow in faith and understanding. When, as a young leader, questions began to emerge about my faith, I was terrified. I was supposed to be the man with the answers. That was my job. I didn't realize that healthy questions strengthen the muscle of faith.

An unquestioning faith, on the other hand, has no depth or resilience and can be a hand-me-down experience in which I just accept ideas because others tell me they are true. Questions are vital. We mustn't dismiss the questioning soul as a cynic or unbeliever. But there are times when we need to suspend our need for answers and just trust in the silent unknowing.

No one dared to ask him who he was, John says.

The word *ask* here means "to interrogate," but this was not the time for detailed, lengthy explanations. There are moments when we just need to put our pressing questions down and simply worship, and we discover that worship and uncertainty can happily coexist.

• • •

A week had gone by without them seeing him.

Our most exhilarating encounters with God can quickly fade, and before long we wonder: Was it really as I said it was? Did that answer to prayer come as I have told it, or in the telling of it, have I managed to convince myself of something that might not be quite true?

Then, suddenly, he returned. There was a sense of awe as well as a hint of uncertainty. John beautifully captures this feeling we often experience when it comes to faith—the sense of realization, or recognition, tinged with disbelief. One writer suggests that the disciples were in a place of saying, "It's you, Jesus. Is it really you, Jesus?" Don Carson puts it this way:

> The disciples had been granted the strongest possible reasons
> for believing in Jesus' resurrection, and indeed did so: they

knew it was the Lord. But whether because they could see Jesus was not simply resuscitated (like Lazarus), but appeared with new powers, or because they were still grappling with the strangeness of a crucified and resurrected Messiah, or because despite the irrefutable power of the evidence presented to them resurrection itself seemed strange, they felt considerable unease—yet suppressed their question because they knew the one before them could only be Jesus.

Sometimes our worship is not so much an expression that comes from a blazing, white-hot furnace of faith, but is rather that of lighting a tiny candle in the midst of the darkness. It is not always the song of those who know, but often the chorus of those who have no clue but trust nevertheless.

These days I'm much more at home with mystery. I used to "know" so much more about God than I do now.

The sea itself speaks of mystery and of us not knowing despite all that we do know. As the disciples huddled together on that shore before Jesus, the sea served as the perfect backdrop for their "unknowing knowing."

Looking toward the horizon, I am possessed of a conceit: with no obstruction in view, I behold so much. I seem to see far into the immensity. It is an illusion. In truth, the full sweep of my sight, from north to south and to the horizon, embraces only a tiny fraction of the ocean's surface. As for what lies beneath, I am blind. I observe no canyons or mountains, no plankton or shrimp or whales. At water's edge, waves of ignorance knock knowledge off its feet. The sea demands humility.... it is unknown and unpredictable and unsafe. One word best describes the sea: mysterious.

As we peer into the invisible realm and by faith see there a king and a kingdom, we're straining to see from our own world, so loaded with very visible, tangible pain and disappointment. Worship is a declaration of hope, sometimes against the apparent odds, and faith-filled worship can surely have hesitation at its heart. Perhaps it always does.

And so initially, the disciples don't have to talk. Some questions would come later, but for now, there was just their togetherness, unspoiled by words.

Yesterday my four-year-old grandson, Stanley, proudly showed me his skills on a scooter. He was insistent, adamant that I offer him my full, undivided attention. "Look at me, Granddad!" he said.

Prayer is partly about talking. Jesus, introducing his model prayer, says, "When you pray, say ..." so words are obviously a component of prayer. But often I have not prayed because I couldn't think of anything sensible to say or was just weary of my own meandering chatter. I'm trying to learn that prayer can be just quietly sitting in the presence of Jesus by faith, not even sanctifying it by straining to listen, but just being with him.

Look at me, Jesus.

And whether I have that uncanny sense of being watched that we experience when we feel eyes are upon us, or if I have no sense of anything at all — if I feel the hint of a smile, or of nothing, faith nudges me to break the silence at last.

It's you, Jesus.

Is it you, Jesus?

7

...

JESUS, I AM NOT IN LOVE WITH YOU

It was full of large fish, 153, but even with so many the net was not torn....

When they had finished eating, Jesus said to Simon Peter, "Simon son of John, do you love me more than these?"

"Yes, Lord," he said, "you know that I love you."

Jesus said, "Feed my lambs."

Again Jesus said, "Simon son of John, do you love me?"

He answered, "Yes, Lord, you know that I love you."

Jesus said, "Take care of my sheep."

The third time he said to him, "Simon son of John, do you love me?"

Peter was hurt because Jesus asked him the third time, "Do you love me?" He said, "Lord, you know all things; you know that I love you."

Jesus said, "Feed my sheep."

JOHN 21:11, 15 – 17

One result of the mysterious nature of love is that no one has ever, to my knowledge, arrived at a truly satisfactory definition of love.

SCOTT PECK

Whenever there's something suspect about an episode that's reported, we say that there's something fishy about it. I'm not sure why. Perhaps it's because of the unjust caricature that fishermen are adept at exaggeration, at describing the elusive "one that got away."

But John 21 is a very fishy story for an altogether different reason: there are a lot of fish in it. Peter had announced his intention to fish, and the outing had proved futile: no fish. Jesus appears, asks for a fishing update, then gives some specific fishing instructions.

They land the catch of their lives, the net copes with the strain, they beach the net, and then it's breakfast time.

I'd like poached eggs and British bacon.

Bacon? This is Israel, so perhaps not.

Okay. I'll take oatmeal, please.

But no options are available, no specific orders being taken for this breakfast. There are just two items on the menu: bread and fish.

There's a whole lot of talk about fish in this story. We're even told precisely how many fish they caught that morning: 153.

Stop right there.

Someone, mercifully unnamed, took the time to count them. The risen Christ is sitting on the beach, and someone is counting fish, perhaps wide-eyed and excited as he does:

78, 79, 80 …

What kind of sad person takes time out from a breakfast with Jesus to count fish?

93, 94, 95 …

Of course, that's what fishermen do. They measure fish and talk about the size of their catch. Modern anglers even fill photograph

albums with snapshots of themselves together with gawping, breathless fish.

103, 104, 105 …

Perhaps it was a prudent thing to do. They'd just experienced a
major miracle—an instant catch gathered at his command. In years
to come, they'd tell the story of that day, prizing the details held in
mind.

Yep, they'd say, we caught a massive catch that morning, and the
skeptic would ask: what exactly do you mean by massive? Precisely
how many fish did you catch, anyway?

149, 150, 151 …

Miracles need to be quantified, evaluated, properly investigated,
don't you know?

It's true. Too many claims are made that God has done something miraculous, leading to disappointment when it turns out that
the claim was enthusiastic but misguided. God is not honored by
stories of things that he allegedly did. Faith loses credibility when we
don't pause and check.

152,… 153!

The fact that the number was recorded has prompted commentators to reach some strange and rather implausible conclusions as
they've tried to make the number 153 significant and symbolic. Some
say that there were 153 languages spoken in the world at that time,
and so each fish represented a nation—that the catch was loaded
with missiological significance.

I don't think so.

Others say that there were 153 different species of fish in the
Sea of Galilee. Really? Why would Jesus want his pals to catch one
of each species?

My favorite suggestion, bizarre in the extreme, is that 153 fish
were caught, because 153 is a triangular number that would have
impressed ancient Pythagorean philosophers. Really? Apparently

Jesus was on a mission to reach tax collectors, sinners, oh, and especially the members of a very small minority group, those ancient Pythagorean philosophers.

Again, I don't think so.

Permit me to offer my own suggestion about this, and brace yourself for a weighty revelation ... or just some hollow speculation. You decide.

Question: Why was it recorded that 153 were caught?

Answer: Because that's how many fish they caught—the catch of their lives.

I know. It's deep. (More about that in a moment.)

Breakfast done, and sharing a little stroll with Peter along the shoreline, Jesus pops the big question: "Simon son of John, do you love me more than these?"

Most think that in this moment, Jesus was glancing at the other disciples, asking Peter if he really loved him more than the other disciples loved him. That might be, but I wonder. Peter had already tried that stunt and failed: Lord, if everyone else denies you, I never will.

Right.

That had lasted about twenty-four hours.

Would Jesus really want Peter to try, once again, to compare himself favorably—or negatively—with the others? How would Peter know how much his friends loved Jesus? So here's a question about that question: Is it just possible that when Jesus said "these" he was referring to fish? Do you love me more than you love fishing?

I'm proposing this not as a statement of fact (nobody can be certain what Jesus was referring to when he said "these"), but as a worthwhile speculation. Is fishing your real, true love, Peter?

I have reasons for my speculation. Peter the fisherman could have enjoyed a quiet life. By doing so, he wouldn't have to be bold and stand up to speak on the day of Pentecost or suffer the indignity and uncertainty of a prison cell. Peter the fisherman would have a predictable, secure life, where there would be no anxieties about church doctrine or conflict, no disappointments when Christian friends let him down, and most of all, no martyrdom at the end of it all. Fishing for Peter meant quiet survival, the humdrum security of an everyday, mundane existence. That could be a significant temptation.

Sometimes I'm lured by the thought of a safe, predictable, even dull existence. I don't want a purpose-driven life. I don't want *purpose*, and I certainly don't want *driven* — I just want a life.

Sometimes I don't want to worry about being responsible about the environment, feeding the hungry, or sharing the good news with the guy next door. Selfishly, I don't want to care about caring anymore. Was Peter tempted by that benign but easy way of life?

There are other hints that Jesus' question was focused around Peter's love for fishing. Peter had been given the new nickname "the rock," but now Jesus gently called Peter by the name that he'd gone by before he'd signed as an apprentice of Christ: Simon son of John. Perhaps Jesus switched back to the old name because he was tenderly nudging Peter to decide who he was going to be from that day forward. Would he be Simon, John's boy, Galilean fisherman — or Peter, friend of Jesus and apostle?

Perhaps there was yet another nudge to Peter's memory as Jesus addressed him this way. In the "rock-renaming" episode, Jesus had used Peter's old name as well as giving him a new one: "Blessed are you, Simon son of Jonah, for this was not revealed to you by flesh and blood, but by my Father in heaven. And I tell you that you are Peter, and on this rock I will build my church, and the gates of Hades will not overcome it."

Is it possible that in addressing Peter this way, Jesus was stirring the weary fisherman not only to remember the day when he had been dubbed "the rock," but also the moment when heaven itself had revealed to Peter the truth that Christ was the Son of God? Would he now live according to that incredible revelation?

And there's another hint. Previously, when Jesus called Peter, he'd used the analogy of fishing as part of that call: "Come, follow me, . . . and I will send you out to fish for people." But now the metaphor that Jesus selects changes from fishing to shepherding. Is it possible that Jesus made this subtle shift because he once again wanted to nudge Peter away from his love of fishing?

It was a huge catch — 153 fish.

But it would never be enough.

Perhaps they got the catch of their lives that day so that they would realize that even a bumper fishing catch wouldn't be enough to satisfy someone who has heard the whisper of heaven. That's why the quiet life, the fruitless existence, will never really work for the Christian.

We've been wonderfully ruined, treated to a vision of the kingdom of God. We've heard the melody of the good news, so the music of mere survival would from then on be a monotonous drone, however hard following Jesus might be at times.

Simon son of John, do you love me more than these?

Whatever Jesus meant when he said "these," the most important question in the world still remained, and Peter struggled to answer it.

Do you love me?

It's a question that I wrestled with in my foggier days, and one that vexes me still at times.

Do I love Jesus?

• • •

Quizzed about what really matters, confronted by a thinly disguised trick question — the most important question, the commandment of commandments — Jesus responded by talking about loving God and neighbor both:

Hearing that Jesus had silenced the Sadducees, the Pharisees got together. One of them, an expert in the law, tested him with this question: "Teacher, which is the greatest commandment in the Law?"

Jesus replied: "'Love the Lord your God with all your heart and with all your soul and with all your mind.' This is the first and greatest commandment. And the second is like it: 'Love your neighbor as yourself.' All the Law and the Prophets hang on these two commandments."

And then there's the compelling and potentially devastating call of Jesus for us to love him more than our nearest and dearest: "Anyone who loves their father or mother more than me is not worthy of me; anyone who loves their son or daughter more than me is not worthy of me."

Those verses really brought the fog down in my darker years. Holding my newborn daughter, Kelly, in my arms for the first time, I had felt a staggering wave of love rise up within me. In that moment, I knew without a shadow of a doubt that I would happily give my life to spare hers. This was raw emotion, but much more: a steely determination to protect her, to seek to do absolutely everything in my power to make her life better, filled my soul.

But it didn't take long for this wave of wonder to be hijacked by another question: did this mean that I loved my daughter more than I loved Jesus? Because I couldn't say, for certain, that I was willing to die for him. And the word *love* was so very confusing. Its meaning has been blurred because we use it in so many ways.

I love Kelly and Richard, my children, Ben, my son-in-law, and I love Stanley and Alex, my grandsons.

I love rich, extravagant sunsets—genius for a few moments, then discarded forever by the dark, allowing the great Artist another attempt tomorrow.

I love the luxurious ice cream we get from my favorite coffee shop in Hawaii, and traditional roast beef Sunday lunches in England, with golden brown potatoes roasted in goose fat.

I love my veteran friendship with Chris and Jeanne; we have shared so many times of laughter and tears.

I love Kay.

But in each of these cases, I am using the word *love* in a uniquely different way. I love Kay, my wife, partly because I can see and touch her. But how do I feel emotionally connected to someone who is currently invisible? And to press the point further, do I have to? What exactly does it mean to love God anyway? And what is love?

In my early years, the fog of confusion was to thicken, especially during worship. At times our songs required me not only to tell Jesus that I loved him, but that I was so in love with him that I wanted to see him, touch him, know him more, see his face, and that he was my lover in what some irreverently tag as "Jesus is my girlfriend" worship songs. And the problem is not just with excessive romanticism and sentimentality, as author and Regent College professor John Stackhouse expresses:

> It's wrong, and I try not to sing wrong lyrics. I'm not in love with Jesus....
>
> Jesus is not your boyfriend, not your fiancé, and not your eventual husband....
>
> So I'm not singing to Jesus that I'm in love with him, because I'm not. I love him, and I aspire to loving him with all my heart, soul, mind, and strength. But I do not aspire to being in love with him, and I'm sure he understands.

For too many years, I tried to fold my soul into having romantic emotions about Jesus. But I am happy, liberated even, to make my own announcement: I too am not in love with Jesus. I love him, and want to love him more, but I am not *in love* with him.

I hear someone protest—what about the Song of Solomon? Isn't that loaded with romantic, even erotic, language?

It is. It's so erotic, some of us have tried to neutralize it by insisting that it's an allegory about God and his people. I think they're wrong. I believe that the Song of Solomon is a book about sex.

The love that Jesus calls us to, that he called Peter to, is not the "in love" kind, with all of the accompanying stomach flutters, daydreaming, and other romanticisms that make being "in love" so delightful—and fleeting, as Scott Peck affirms:

When a person falls in love he or she certainly feels, "I love him" or "I love her." But two problems are immediately apparent. The first is that the experience of falling in love is specifically a sex-linked erotic experience. We do not fall in love with our children even though we may love them very deeply. We do not fall in love with our friends of the same sex—unless we are homosexually oriented—even though we may care for them greatly. We fall in love only when we are consciously or unconsciously sexually motivated. The second problem is that the experience of falling in love is invariably temporary. No matter whom we fall in love with, we sooner or later fall out of love if the relationship continues long enough. This is not to say that we invariably cease loving the person with whom we fell in love. But it is to say that the feeling of ecstatic lovingness that characterizes the experience of falling in love always passes. The honeymoon always ends. The bloom of romance always fades.

Perhaps that's why I find myself wanting to sing more songs about who and what God is—his attributes that are unchanging, regardless of the emotional or circumstantial weather that I'm experiencing.

Christianity is a relationship with God that is conducted by faith. We can't see him, touch him, and hear him much of the time, so there's a danger of even lifting the relationship that Jesus had, while on this earth, with human beings that he knew, and then trying to replicate the terms of those relationships exactly in our own experience today.

Let me illustrate.

This is the usual way that preachers approach narratives like this:

Jesus wanted to know if Peter loved him, because Peter's love for Jesus was the most important issue. In the same way, God wants us to know if we love him. So do we?

There's one problem.

Peter was Jesus' friend in a unique way. They were together for three years. They walked dusty roads, shared ten thousand conversations together, laughed and cried, forged memories and shared disappointments. Peter knew Jesus, discovered things about Jesus that he especially liked and loved. There was a human-to-human affection between the two.

And that's where things are different for me: Jesus and I haven't actually met yet.

One day that will all change with a face-to-face encounter. But in the meantime I don't know him in the way that I know Kay or Kelly or Richard or Ben. And so I don't have to try to contort myself to manufacture the same feelings of love that I have for all of them in my relationship by faith with Jesus.

That's not to say that Christianity isn't emotional or that it's a cold, sterile belief system. On the contrary, I experience joy in the belief that I am rescued, gratitude for amazing provision, sorrow when I let him down, relief when I am forgiven, delight in the experience of being part of his family. But I don't have to feel shame when those feelings are absent, because it's probable that even when Jesus was quizzing his face-to-face friend Peter, he wasn't asking about how Peter felt about him at all, but rather, if Peter would live for him.

When Jesus reaffirmed the first commandment, calling us to love God with everything we have, he uses a word rich in meaning: the verb *agapao*. To love.

To *agapao* something means to totally give ourselves over to it, to be totally consumed with it—or to be totally committed to it. What we *agapao* is what we put first in our lives.

Here's what Scott Peck has to say on the act of love:

> Love is an action, an activity ... love is not a feeling. Many, many people possessing a feeling of love and even acting in response to that feeling act in all manner of unloving and destructive ways. On the other hand, a genuinely loving individual will often take loving and constructive action toward a person he or she consciously dislikes, actually feeling no love toward the person at the time and perhaps even finding the person repugnant in some way.

Peter was about to be asked to show action, not just feeling-based love. But before that, an interesting conversation ensued, one that commentators have argued over for centuries.

• • •

I've never taken a lie detector test, and wonder how I would do if placed in that pressurized environment. There have been times when I've even wondered if my prayers would pass as truth or lies.

Sometimes I turn prayer into a speech—and not just when others are listening. In my mind and with my lips, I say things to God that sound right, as if he is pleased merely with the pleasant arrangement of words. But God knows our hearts anyway and isn't impressed when we try to disguise what we really feel with pious language.

When Jesus asked Peter if he truly loved him, Peter responded cautiously—the word he uses means "I am fond of you." Commentators have debated this switch between *agape* love and *phileo* love endlessly; some say that it is significant that Peter carefully deliberated over his response because he wanted to be authentic. Others dismiss this because the two words used here—agape and phileo—were used interchangeably in the Greek language anyway, especially in John's gospel, so we shouldn't read too much into the dialogue.

While it's uncertain, perhaps Peter was being very careful. He'd been rather good at allowing words to tumble out of his mouth, words that he hadn't thought through; perhaps the humbled, penitent Peter is much more careful about rushing in with hasty promises. Now Jesus is looking not for a swift profession of commitment, but for an authentic expression of love: Do you truly love me? Peter rightly hesitated and tried to be as honest as he could about the state of his heart.

If Peter had amended his words, professing "agape" love instead of strong affection, surely he would have shown that he hadn't learned from his mistakes. Better to stay honest, Peter, and authentic with it, than resort to platitudes that might please anyone except Jesus, who can see through it all anyway. I don't think of this as a test, but if it had been, Peter surely passed with flying colors because, quite simply, he told the truth.

But when Jesus dug further with his questions—his surgery going deeper—Peter was hurt. The word used here for hurt is quite strong, meaning grief, sometimes with tears. With all that we have hopefully seen about the loving tenderness of Jesus in these pages, we need to remember that he is not afraid of causing us pain if we will ultimately benefit from it.

God disciplines us not because of any lack of love, but because he loves us. He cares so intensely that he won't just allow us to meander into disaster without challenging us in a way that we might find painful. But it really is for our good, to bring us to a place of self-awareness.

Grace doesn't mean that Jesus is some kind of benevolent Santa Claus who exists solely to make us happy. He is committed to our transformation and to us achieving our potential—and that will mean some rebukes and chastening along the way. And self-deception, where we refuse to face up to our frailties and justify our sins with what sounds like reasonable excuses, is a dangerous tumor that calls for the surgeon's knife.

Jesus is supremely skilled at these operations and loves his patients. And so there was comfort as well as cutting in this particular procedure.

• • •

Jesus asked Peter the same question three times. It's not a usual social practice to put the same question to someone repeatedly. Doing so suggests that we either doubt their honesty or, perhaps, are hard of hearing.

So why the "do you love me?" inquiry three times? Some think that Jesus offered Peter the opportunity to express his love for Jesus in triplicate because he had denied Christ three times. Others note that when something was said three times in Near Eastern culture, it became legally binding; this was a solemn vow as well as a firm calling from Jesus to Peter to become a shepherd in the flock of God.

Perhaps Jesus choreographed this conversation because he wanted to drive home to Peter the fact that his love was accepted and that his calling was real. Maybe he wanted Peter to know beyond any doubt that some very tough times lay ahead. Time tends to erode even the most amazing experiences; it was vital that Peter would never ever forget his fireside chat.

He really was accepted.

Paul Tillich states the following:

You are accepted. You are accepted, accepted by that which is greater than you, and the name of which you do not know. Do not ask for the name now; perhaps you will find it later. Do not try to do anything now; perhaps later you will do much. Do not seek for anything; do not perform anything; do not intend anything. Simply accept the fact that you are accepted! If that happens to us, we experience grace. After such an experience we may not be better than before, and we may not believe more than before. But everything is transformed. In that moment, grace conquers sin, and reconciliation bridges the gulf of estrangement. And nothing is demanded of this experience, no religious or moral or intellectual presupposition, nothing but acceptance.

Perhaps Tillich overstates his case, as grace does ultimately lead to mission, responsibility, and action. Peter, expressing his love for Christ, was given a task. But Tillich's point is well made, because how often do we rush to action without the issue of our absolute acceptance being settled? Then our work, instead of being grateful worship offered in response to God's unmerited favor, becomes sweaty, anxious striving as we desperately try to gain God's favor.

And so not only is Peter accepted—he then found that he was trusted again.

When we fail miserably, especially after promising absolute faithfulness, we usually feel unworthy of trust. Why should the person we've failed bother to believe that we are going to change? The past is a good indicator of future performance, or so they say, and so failure renders us feeling not only ashamed, but useless—rejected as being unpredictable and therefore not to be trusted.

When Jesus told Peter to shepherd the flock of God, surely he was not just responding to Peter's "I'm fond of you" affirmation with a blunt "prove it, work for me" answer. At first glance it could appear that way. It is true that obedience is the major way that we demonstrate our love for Jesus. If you love me, keep my commands. That's certainly clear and to the point. But surely Jesus was giving Peter the very beautiful gift of trust.

The man who probably felt so useless was once again being invited to take a vital role in Christ's kingdom purposes; now his heart was warmed by the truth that his miserable fickleness hadn't canceled out his calling. Rita F. Snowden writes, "You ask me what forgiveness means. It is the wonder of being trusted again by God in the place where I disgraced Him."

We might struggle and protest that we're too messed up or lacking in love—but his calling to us comes with his complete and total knowledge of who we are. He doesn't include us as his partners for the kingdom despite our frailties, but rather with full knowledge of them.

Peter had denied Jesus with curses. When we think about that episode, we tend to focus upon how this affected Peter rather than the effect of his disloyalty upon Jesus.

If someone had wounded me so terribly, there would be a whole host of questions to be answered:

Why did you do it?

Will you betray me again?

How can I trust you now that I know how unstable you can be?

I even warned you this would happen—didn't you take any notice of what I said?

Or perhaps before reinstating Peter to leadership, I'd interrogate him carefully to try to discern if his repentance was authentic: Was he sorry because he was embarrassed and ashamed, or was he truly remorseful?

If Jesus talked about any of these issues with Peter, Scripture doesn't record it, but Jesus again trusted him. He also trusted him with a knowledge that most of us would never want.

Jesus was about to tell Peter just how he would die.

• • •

Before we move on, a confession: I'm unsure how I would have answered Jesus' questions if I'd been in Peter's sandals. Perhaps like Peter, the question would cause me to stammer because I too don't trust myself enough to be able to profess that I absolutely love God without any sense of hesitation. How do I know?

Am I deceiving myself, loving the work that I do more than the God whom I am supposed to be working for?

If feelings aren't the barometer, then how do I measure my love for him or know whether I am growing to love him more as the days go by?

It's then my heart often condemns me.

In the end, Peter offers his love but qualifies his words by affirming that, ultimately, Jesus knew everything anyway. We offer what love we have, knowing that he alone knows what's really true. John, "the disciple whom Jesus loved," offers assurance in his epistle, especially to the one who experiences condemnation: "This is how we know that we belong to the truth and how we set our hearts at rest in his presence: If our hearts condemn us, we know that God is greater than our hearts, and he knows everything."

That's where I set my own heart at rest; I want to love God more but don't really know how to definitively authenticate or measure my love for him. Ironically, my angst is evidence of love: the fact that I am concerned about my love for God is proof that I love him. But ultimately, I can't sort it all out. Like Peter, I mumble my love.

But he knows me. He is the great One.

I'll trust his verdict.

8

• • •

MAKING GOD
LOOK GOOD

Jesus said, "Feed my sheep. Very truly I tell you, when you were younger you dressed yourself and went where you wanted; but when you are old you will stretch out your hands, and someone else will dress you and lead you where you do not want to go." Jesus said this to indicate the kind of death by which Peter would glorify God.

JOHN 21:17–19

It must be realized that the true sign of spiritual endeavor and the price of success in it is suffering. One who proceeds without suffering will bear no fruit ... every struggle in the soul's training, whether physical or mental, that is not accompanied by suffering, that does not require the utmost effort, will bear no fruit ... many people have worked and continue to work without pain, but because of its absence they are strangers to purity.

THEOPHAN THE RECLUSE

All the great religions were first preached, and long practiced, in a world without chloroform.

C. S. LEWIS

Breakfast was over. Stomachs were full, hearts warmed, and a vital, life-changing conversation had unfolded. Love had been affirmed once again. Grace was in the air. The bleak horizon that shame had created for Peter was fading, and now a world of possibilities was beginning to open to him once more. He'd been reinstated and much more.

But many questions must have been forming.

Shepherding the sheep—what did that mean? What would it look like?

What sheep?

Now what?

Where are you going, Jesus, and when?

What part will you play in all of this?

There would be countless conversations between them in the six-week period until he ascended. But for now, at least, there's no mention of the day of Pentecost to come, of the need for Peter to stand up and say this or that—to be strong. There's no briefing for that day yet.

There's no dialogue either about thousands suddenly choosing to be disciples at the end of Peter's maiden sermon.

No promise of supernatural power pulsating as his shadow passed over the sick.

No conversation yet about the epic part that Peter would play in church and world history, just that amazing commission: shepherd and feed my sheep.

For now, the next item on the agenda is a warning from Jesus, one that Peter will live with for three decades. Just one stunning sentence that he would recall again and again. Perhaps years later, he would try to remember the tone of Jesus' voice, certain and sober, yet tender still.

Be assured, there's trouble ahead. You're free to come and go as you please now, Peter, but one day that will change. There will be prison. And after that, Peter, your execution.

You'll die a martyr.

Breakfast ended with the assurance, if we can describe it so, that a death sentence was in the future. Days earlier, Peter had pledged his life to Jesus, promised faithfully that he was ready to go both to prison and to death for Christ. That iron resolve of his had lasted less than twenty-four hours; perhaps he thought that Jesus' warning about the denials to come meant that he was totally dismissing his pledge. But now, what had seemed like a vacuous promise to endure jail and death was being called in by Jesus. He was extending an invitation to walk a pathway of pain, and the events of the Easter weekend meant that Peter knew from close observation exactly what prison and death would look and feel like.

Peter had no desire to taste captivity, and now, incarceration and execution were being promised, prophesied by Jesus. Peter would have had no doubt that whatever Jesus predicted would come to pass. He'd told them clearly about his trial, death, and resurrection, all plainly set out before the event.

Incredibly, it had happened exactly as he said.

He'd specially told Peter that he would be buffeted, sifted like wheat as Satan sought to unsettle him. The events of the last few weeks had proven that to be exactly right. His denial had happened exactly as Jesus had said. He'd even predicted the number of times that Peter would deny him before the rooster crowed in the early morning hours.

He would never forget the sound of that rooster as long as he lived. And surely he would wake up every day with the latest prediction on his mind too: Suffering and martyrdom were ahead. Of that he could be certain.

It was promised.

• • •

Suffering.

It's thought to be the Achilles heel for the Christian. The New Atheists, whose insistence that science trumps faith, lecture and write prolifically about a world full of pain and insist that the evil that apparently runs rampant cancels out the possibility of a God. If there is an Almighty, why are we in such an almighty mess? The perennial question torments: Why do bad things happen to good people?

Suffering.

It's supposed to erode faith, even among the vintage faithful. When tragedy strikes, the most reasonable, logical thing to do is to abandon God, either by ignoring him or writing off his existence altogether—or so goes the reasoning. After all, even if there is such a thing as God, apparently he has tossed us aside and left us at the mercy of chance, ill winds, or bad luck.

Some of the strongest believers I've met have developed a titanium-strength trust in God as they've navigated through awful seasons of suffering. Pain has not weakened their grip on God; rather, it's strengthened it. I listen as they whisper their stories of agonizing loss, and, feeling unworthy, I bow my head in the presence of such epic conviction.

A stunning prayer was prayed amid the horrors of Ravensbrück concentration camp, built by the Nazis in 1939 to house and then exterminate women. Over 90,000 women and children perished there. Corrie ten Boom, who wrote *The Hiding Place*, was incarcerated there. The prayer, found in the clothing of a dead child, says:

O Lord, remember not only the men and women of good will, but also those of ill will. But do not remember all of the suffering they have inflicted upon us:

Instead remember the fruits we have borne because of this suffering, our fellowship, our loyalty to one another, our humil-

ity, our courage, our generosity, the greatness of heart that has
grown from this trouble.

When our persecutors come to be judged by you, let all of
these fruits that we have borne be their forgiveness.

I am both inspired and totally intimidated by such towering
trust.

As a fledgling minister, working hard to plant a church within a
needy housing project, I encountered shades of suffering every day in
others; and as I watched good, godly people suffer, the fog swirled in.

Lone parents battled to bring up teenagers on budgets that barely
kept them fed, never mind provided them with the latest necessities.
Faithful souls popped in to see the doctor with a niggling ache or
pain and emerged twenty minutes later with a likely death sentence,
cancer cells conspiring to end their godly lives prematurely. Others battled with long-term unemployment. In some cases they were
so, but even if a job surfaced, they were extremely unlikely to find
themselves in work. Their economic future looked bleak, with all the
difficulties associated with near poverty.

And then, those very same souls would huddle together for
warmth on Sunday mornings, and we would sing bright songs about
joy and God's power and love, and they would file their way to the
front of the church and request prayer, hoping somehow that things
might be different: that money would come, that the vile tumor
would be vaporized, that a job would surface.

And I would tell them that God was indeed mighty.

I believed it then, and I still do now. But it was difficult to hold
onto the possibility of intervention, of healing, of provision, of
employment, when it generally felt like it was faith against the odds.
Real change seemed unlikely.

It would have been easier to believe that God never heals today
than walk through the agonizing possibility that he sometimes does.

Talking day after day about supernatural intervention—when, to be frank, most prayers seemed to be met with indifference—was tough indeed. Balancing the tension between belief that God is active and helping people live in circumstances that seemed to deny that truth was difficult.

On some days, it felt like an impossibility.

This is bad, Pastor, they'd say, recounting the terrible news from their hospital appointment.

God is big, I'd retort. He is able, I'd say. He might do something, I'd think. Possibly. Maybe. We hope so, and we pray so. Here are the promises of God that say that he cares for us. Hold onto them tightly, as you trek your weary way to another session of chemotherapy.

Life seemed random, unplanned, certainly ungoverned by any sovereign hand. Trying to help people walk through long-term, agonizing terminal illness, there were times when the promises of God seemed hollow. I really wanted to believe that prayer meant that suffering could be avoided. Ignoring the promise of Jesus that life in this world involves trouble, I viewed the promises of God as evidence that we could avoid pain and suffering.

That same notion leads some to believe that if we're not spared suffering, then something's wrong, and if God is beyond being wrong, then the fault must be with us—and that's when fog really rolls in.

• • •

News had broken during a major Christian conference in the UK that an extremely popular and gifted speaker was in the clutches of a cancer. The prognosis was bleak, the medics had exhausted all their options, and he, a husband and father of very young children, had been sent home to die. He and his family had responded to the situation with a deep, authentic trust in God.

Back at the conference, a special prayer meeting was called to cry out to God for healing. The prayers were loud and fervent, and

those who gathered were deeply sincere, fueled by love and desperation. With tears and raised voices, we implored God to rise up, break
chains, banish disease, and send Satan packing. But then one person
offered a prayer that I was uncomfortable with: "I simply refuse to
accept that this is going to end in death."

That's when we tipped into the grey zone, because suffering
often causes us to detach from reality. We scramble for fixes and solutions, and proffer slogans that simply aren't true. But still they keep
being rehearsed in local churches everywhere, every time another
Christian gets seriously ill or experiences a major tragedy. Christians
often inflict great pain on each other when they resort to these well-
meaning but hollow slogans:

Faith is not believing that God will do something; it is knowing
that he will do something, say some.

But much of the time we don't know what he's going to do — or
not do, as the case may be. Some, with the best intentions, cause
great pain by promising that God will heal, rescue, or intervene, only
to discover that he did not. When that happens, we turn to more
desperate measures to explain our quandary.

We didn't pray enough.

Really? Does God have some kind of meter that allows him to
measure how many people have prayed? ("Sorry, we needed the full
quota of 11,234 people praying in order for Mrs. Smith to get well.
But we were fifty intercessors short. Request denied.")

You're sick because you don't have enough faith, insist others.

Great. Not only do I feel desperately unwell, but I've got a bigger
issue as one who doubts.

Undeniably, in the ministry of Jesus, faith — or more specifically,
unbelief — affected his ability to work miracles. But to rush to the
conclusion that a person is not healed because of their lack of faith is
a huge presumption. Who are we to say who has faith and who does
not, and whether or not faith was an issue at all?

Still others, acting as self-appointed prosecuting attorneys, say there's sin in your life.

Recently I met a young mother who was told by her Christian friends (who were perhaps descended from those "comforters" that Job had to put up with) that the terminal disease that was ravaging her child was because of some secret sin in her life. Let's call this what it is: spiritual abuse, adding a heap of condemnation to her crushing distress and mind-altering anxiety.

Other "helpers" head in another direction, suggesting passive resignation is the best way to respond to pain: God planned this suffering. It's God's will.

But not everything that happens is God's will. Just because Jesus predicted Peter's imprisonment and death doesn't mean that he planned it, any more than predicting Peter's threefold denial meant that it was part of some huge master blueprint. God doesn't always get his will done; that's why we're taught to pray your kingdom come, your will be done. The universe is not spinning out of control, because God is working on the big picture; but he has determined that his sovereignty is not expressed in every tiny detail, turning the world into a puppet theater where everything that happens is because of a divine pull on the strings.

Our hollow slogans prove that we Christians, at least in the comfortable Western Hemisphere, generally don't do so well when it's time to suffer. In some churches, even sickness is a badge of shame. I know of believers who have trudged the shadowy pathway of terminal illness, who didn't ever get to say goodbye to their loved ones because it would have been tantamount to admitting defeat. Some of them died with a sense of failure and loneliness.

One lovely Christian man didn't want to tell people in his church that he'd been given a terminal prognosis. He didn't want to disappoint the team of intercessors who'd been praying for him.

But we're never promised that we won't suffer. On the contrary, we are promised that we will.

The statistics are impressive: one out of every one people die. Until Jesus returns, none of us are going to get out of this life alive.

We'll lose people we love.

Unexplainable things happen.

And so Peter had to face the future with his eyes wide open. There was trouble ahead. And glory with it.

• • •

Back on the beach, Jesus had given Peter a harrowing promise of a martyr's death, but the promise came with a bizarre addendum: In dying this way, Peter would be privileged to glorify God.

Suffering and glory entwined was a strange, unwelcome gift. It's not one that most of us want to receive, even if Scripture is emphatic: the link between suffering and solid-gold, God-glorifying faith is undeniable.

Later, as he shepherded the sheep, Peter would teach about the link between the words *suffering* and *glory*. No wonder. It was a truth indelibly burned into his heart and mind, a reality that he would live and die in too.

For a little while you may have had to suffer grief in all kinds of trials. These have come so that the proven genuineness of your faith—of greater worth than gold, which perishes even though refined by fire—may result in praise, glory and honor when Jesus Christ is revealed.

If you are insulted because of the name of Christ, you are blessed, for the Spirit of glory and of God rests on you. If you suffer, it should not be as a murderer or thief or any other kind of criminal, or even as a meddler. However, if you suffer as a Christian, do not be ashamed, but praise God that you bear that name.

And again:

> To the elders among you, I appeal as a fellow elder and a
> witness of Christ's sufferings who also will share in the glory
> to be revealed.

Here's the wonderful and perhaps unpalatable connection between glory and suffering that emerges in what Peter lived and what he had to say: his own faithfulness to Jesus, all the way to and through martyrdom, would bring glory to God. Genuine, enduring faith glorifies God now and will do so in the future, when Christ comes. The "Spirit of glory" rests on us as we suffer. And at the end of everything, we will share in the "glory to be revealed."

I want to live a life that makes God look good. That may sound rather crude, but the essence of glorifying God is living in a way that shows his beautiful character so that others don't merely admire him, but get to know him. Glorifying God doesn't just mean that we strut through life sporting dozens of answers to prayer, experiencing victory over every sickness and disease, and generally being a walking, talking demonstration of what the power of God could do.

Sure, Peter experienced that power — but he would also glorify God in his infirmity, imprisonment, and death. It would not be by escaping pain that Peter would bring glory to the name of Jesus, but rather as he lived in tenacious faithfulness despite the cost.

That's why I've bumped into some of the greatest faith not in high-powered, excited healing services, but in cancer wards, and as I've met people who have stayed faithful through other terrible tragedies. Far from being defeated, they've been victorious by clinging tightly to Jesus by faith, even in the midst of mayhem. Their endurance speaks volumes about the faithfulness and grace of God that is available to us in the darkest of days. As Jesus glorified the Father through his faithfulness, and ultimately his obedience to the death, so those who call themselves his followers will often find themselves walking a similar pathway.

• • •

What did it feel like for Peter to live out the rest of his life with the sure knowledge that his end would be a martyr's death? I think if I'd been him, I might have been tempted to stop Jesus halfway through his sentence:

Enough Lord. If it's alright with you, I'd rather not know.

But now he knew.

Did Peter ask Jesus for more information? When would it happen, this martyrdom? Would his family still be alive at that terrible time? What would become of them?

Jesus said it wouldn't take place until Peter was old — so if he was to live a long life, would it be productive and fruitful? But if Jesus gave Peter any further insight and information about his future, we're not told.

Peter was called not only to put his faith into action, but to be incredibly faithful in the midst of so many questions. And so are we.

Tradition has it that Peter literally "stretched out his hands" and was crucified, probably during the Emperor Nero's reign in about AD 64. Many legends surround his death, including him being crucified upside down. Some say this was at his own request, because he did not feel worthy to suffer in the same way that Jesus did. Other rumors say that it took him three days to die.

None of these can be substantiated, and Scripture is silent on the subject, perhaps because it is more important to know about faithfulness in suffering than to know the details of the suffering itself. But however it happened, the chilling prediction came true.

And Peter was faithful to the end, not only as a martyr, but in three decades of knowing that he would be a martyr.

But in the meantime, there was much to be done.

9

• • •

FOLLOW ME?

Then he said to him, "Follow me!"

JOHN 21:19

The fourth step of humility is accepting the hardships of the commandments and enduring with patience the injuries and afflictions we face. We are called to endure and not grow weary or give up, but to hold fast. The Scriptures teach us, "They that persevere unto the end shall be saved."

ST. BENEDICT

Does the road wind up-hill all the way?
Yes, to the very end.
Will the day's journey take the whole long day?
From morn to night, my friend.

CHRISTINA ROSSETTI

I cannot read. I cannot think. I cannot even pray.
But I can trust.

HUDSON TAYLOR, in the midst of a nervous breakdown,
when told that fifty-eight missionaries and their twenty-one
children had been killed in the Chinese Boxer Revolution

Follow me.

Just two words.

But those words had triggered a revolution in Peter's life three years earlier. And absolutely everything changed for him when he responded to Jesus' invitation. In issuing the call, Jesus laid out no route map and outlined no detailed plans. It really was a leap of faith for Peter.

The call was not to go somewhere, but rather to be with someone, and so all Peter knew was that he was being invited to be with this marvelous, mysterious Jesus, and that from then on he'd "fish for men."

Now that's a strange but tantalizing job description.

In the heady three years that followed, Peter experienced so many emotions: Everest summits when revelations dawned on him without warning; Death Valleys of despair as he'd battled bewilderment and disappointment—mainly with himself.

He'd tried hard to make sense of the unpredictable friend and rabbi who stood with him there on the beach. Jesus had been like a mirror to Peter, showing him the uncomfortable and, at times, ugly truth. Jesus had unlocked the very secrets of the universe to this Galilean fisherman. And now, there was blood on the horizon.

If Peter could have caught the slightest glimpse of what was unfolding for him in world history, he would have been staggered. As he and Jesus strolled along the beach, the sun slowly inching higher in the day, Peter was a history maker in the making. But he didn't know that then and certainly couldn't grasp the fullness of what that looked like.

There had been moments of decision before, times when he could have just walked away, abandoned the rabbi, gone back to the family business, and gotten on with his life. But when a whole swathe of Jesus' followers had decided to abandon him, appalled by some of his sayings, Peter and the eleven had decided to stick with him.

> On hearing it, many of his disciples said, "This is a hard teaching. Who can accept it?"
>
> Aware that his disciples were grumbling about this, Jesus said to them, "Does this offend you? Then what if you see the Son of Man ascend to where he was before! The Spirit gives life; the flesh counts for nothing. The words I have spoken to you—they are full of the Spirit and life. Yet there are some of you who do not believe." For Jesus had known from the beginning which of them did not believe and who would betray him. He went on to say, "This is why I told you that no one can come to me unless the Father has enabled them."
>
> From this time many of his disciples turned back and no longer followed him.
>
> "You do not want to leave too, do you?" Jesus asked the Twelve.
>
> Simon Peter answered him, "Lord, to whom shall we go? You have the words of eternal life. We have come to believe and to know that you are the Holy One of God."

Peter had himself pledged ongoing commitment to Jesus when many were walking away.

Perhaps he made his confession of faithfulness with a firm voice and sparkling eyes. Or did he pledge allegiance with mixed feelings—a statement of faith made with a shrug of the shoulders, a sigh of resignation, a dogged determination to go with what was right regardless of how he felt? It must have been tough to see so many leave. Were those who walked away all deluded and the few that stayed behind so enlightened? Should he vote with his feet too?

When Jesus had announced his fateful decision to head for the intimidating city of Jerusalem, Peter and the others had opted to go with him, despite an ominous atmosphere that lingered at that time. Thomas, sadly more famous for doubting than bravery, made a courageous pledge: "Let us also go, that we may die with him."

But now another juncture moment had arrived. The past was the past, and it was becoming increasingly obvious that Jesus would not be with Peter and his friends in person much longer. Everything was changing. Within weeks, Jesus would be going away.

From then on, Peter would be walking with Jesus — not at all in the way he had, but rather in the way that we do. He would continue to communicate with the man who had presided over the miraculous breakfast, but through prayer, a fantastic, bewildering concept for Peter to grasp, if indeed he'd even begun to grapple with it at this stage. No longer would he see that familiar face; instead, he would have to trust that his friend and rabbi still heard him: a walk of faith.

It's one thing to suffer when you've got Jesus right there at your side, steering you, correcting you, comforting you. Jesus. Close. It's quite another challenge to walk into a painful future with the knowledge that he would not be there in the same way at all.

Another "comforter" was coming to take his place, Jesus said. The Holy Spirit. Did Peter think: Thanks, but no thanks? You stay, Jesus; you're who we want.

No wonder Jesus constantly assured his friends that he was going to be with them always. Their greatest fear was realized because, having gone away from them once, to the cross and to death, now he was going away again.

The disciples were becoming apostles, moving into an entirely different phase of their mission — and Peter was being shaped, perhaps to his surprise, to assume the role of key leader of the little apostolic band. And so with the additional news that it would ultimately cost him life itself, the old call—the very same invitation—was renewed again for Peter: follow me.

Yesterday's pledges were not sufficient for this totally new phase. Jesus sought a fresh response, not least because the promise that Jesus made was quite radically different: three years earlier, Peter had been promised that he'd fish for men.

Now, another promise: death.

Are you still up for this, Peter?

Everything was different. It had been here, on the Sea of Galilee, that Peter had walked on the water to reach Jesus—and sank, dunked by his fears. Today, he'd had to wade through the water to get to Jesus.

Walking on water.

Walking through water.

I know which I'd prefer.

• • •

It was a rather tame experiment, but I once tried to walk on water. Staying at a hotel that was relatively deserted, I found myself quite alone at the side of the swimming pool. And so I decided to try my walking-on-water experiment. Of course, it was nothing like Peter's epic—but brief—march across windswept, boiling waves. I tried to cross the millpond-still (and pleasantly warm) water of a pool.

And I did opt for a swimsuit. Looking this way and that to make sure I was not being watched, I prayed for a moment or two, then stepped onto the surface of the water—and promptly sank. A failed mission.

But this much I know: walking on water looks like a lot more fun than walking through it. Peter had known the exhilaration of placing his foot on a wave and finding that it, impossibly, supported his weight. But everything changed, and he had to content himself with wading through water to get to the beach where Jesus had been waiting.

Perhaps we've known better times in the past, seasons of great breakthrough, when prayer was invariably answered and it seemed that whatever we touched turned to gold. We felt like we could walk on water.

But now the blue sky has been replaced by cloudier days; summer has turned into an autumnal season. The question is this: Will we still be faithful and love Jesus now, even if walking through water is what is needed?

Will we still follow?

Everything was different in Peter too. He had been changed by the last three years. Some of his confidence had been knocked out by his failures; these days he took a little more time to engage his heart and brain before opening his mouth. He was not the same man who had heard that call three years earlier.

And it's true for us too. It's not just that our circumstances change as the years roll by; we change too. The person who "gave his life" to Christ at the tender age of seventeen is not the same person that I am today. In fact, the two are probably barely recognizable as the same person.

So what now?

• • •

When I decided to become a follower of Christ, my life experience was virtually nil. Growing up, I'd never been encouraged to think much about ambition or purpose. There were no mealtime conversations about politics, philosophy, or religion. The assumption was that I would graduate from high school and get a job with the same elevator company that my father, brother, uncle, and cousin worked for, a multinational business that nevertheless felt like the family firm to me. I would become an elevator maintenance engineer.

College was out of the question, and not just for financial reasons. It was simply never a subject that was discussed. In those days, children took an examination at the age of eleven, the "eleven plus." Those who passed were sent to grammar school and were groomed for higher education. Those who failed were sent to secondary schools and were destined for the blue-collar workforce, although that had begun to change at about the time I went into the system.

I took the eleven plus test and failed. Secondary school for me.

And so, in my thinking, it was the other people — the middle- and upper-class people, and those who passed that examination — who were the ones who went to university.

My only excursion into political conversation came when I got a part-time job as an assistant stage manager in a London-based Marxist theatre company. Within weeks I started talking about workers' rights and revolutions, despite have absolutely no knowledge of Marxist ideology whatsoever. I just gleaned enough from the conversations of the actors and stage crew to fuel my chatter. And because I was desperate to fit in, my desire to belong drove me to naively accept their ideas. I liked them, and so I assumed that they were right.

When I became a Christian some months later, having had an undeniable encounter with God, I accepted the Christian message, as it was presented to me, without question or hesitation. The person who led me in what we would now call "the sinner's prayer" gave me a little booklet that outlined the basics of Christian belief, and as I took the booklet in hand, I fully accepted its contents without reflection, question, or evaluation.

The process was as simple as this:

Something stunning had happened to me (a healing) that I could only assume was God at work (only God could do that).

I had then bumped into a group of people who claimed to know God, who then told me that I could know him too.

Keen to know God, I accepted what they had to say.

My Christian faith was as straightforward as that for the first couple of years. Even my time at Bible College, preparing for ministry—which should have been a time of theological sifting and careful reflection—didn't serve that purpose, through nobody's fault but my own. Blinded by a passionate desire to reach the world, I treated my studies with disdain, telling myself that I didn't need all that knowledge, but that God's calling and power would suffice. How foolish and headstrong I was, and my ignorant passion set me up, partially, for my later depression.

Before long, I started to question some of the doctrines that I had so quickly accepted. Not only was I somewhat bewildered by the questions that were arising, but I didn't have the intellectual and theological apparatus to handle them. I panicked, fearing that I was losing my faith, that everything that I had given my life for to that point was all a waste of time.

Ministry also brought bumps and bruises. I had fallen in love with the church the day that I became a Christian, but now that love was certainly being tested. And then there was the fact that I was growing up.

The late teenager was now in his mid-twenties, a husband and a father. I began to lose my naivety. Invited to speak at some interdenominational Christian conferences, I was shocked to discover that there were others whose theology was different from mine and my denomination's, but they loved Jesus with passion and energy.

Also, the fact that I had become a Christian as a teenager began to bother me. Had I swallowed the beliefs of Christians as quickly as I had parroted some of the mantras of Marxism back in my theatre days? My time as a trainee Marxist had not lasted too long. Would I find myself abandoning my Christianity too, writing it off as a childish, unsustainable phase?

I genuinely feared cynicism. Unable to differentiate between skepticism, which is healthy, and cynicism, which is so destructive, I battled to stay open on the one hand and yet not dive headfirst into foolishness on the other.

What was real?

Now I understood why Scripture says so much not just about beginnings, but about ending in faith. We often think that new Christians are the ones who are the most vulnerable, and discipleship courses and structures are rightly provided to help new converts in their inductive years. But Scripture has much to say about faithfulness, endurance, and maintaining our first love for Christ.

I had assumed that the New Testament is mainly concerned about conversion, grounding new Christians, and establishing them—getting them going, if you will. But I had neglected to see that much of the time Scripture is directed to help disciples keep going—maintaining longevity and finishing well.

It's easy to start something.

A new project.

A groundbreaking initiative.

There's anticipation, the buzz of strategic conversations, the joy of meeting obstacles and challenges head-on:

A New Year's resolution. A diet.

A new version of you. Being able to buy those clothes that you've wanted to wear for years. Abandoning black simply because it's slimming. Going swimming with pride rather than shame.

A discipline. Armed with that shiny new gym membership card, you're eager to hit the treadmill.

Starting the Christian life is easy. Keeping going and finishing is something else.

Ask any marathon runner. There's sweat. Pain. Hitting the wall. Your mind at times screaming, "Give up!" It's no wonder that running is one of the favorite New Testament analogies for the Christian life.

But runners dream of the tape, of crossing the finish line. And you take another step.

...

The life that I offered to Jesus all those years ago is not the life I have now.

I am hurtling at terrifying speed toward a birthday with a number 6 in it, which is a surprise to me. And like most who are getting older, I'm in disbelief at the ridiculous speed of the process, for I still feel like an eighteen-year-old trapped in an aging body, who wonders what on earth has happened.

I was especially unprepared for what took place in just one period of my life that spanned 132 months. One day I was thirty-nine, a relatively young man. Just eleven years later, I woke up to discover that I was now a man in his early fifties. In a little over 500 weeks, everything changed, the rudest of awakenings. I am utterly different.

But I believe in what I cannot see.

Because I came to faith with naivety doesn't make the truth any less true. God has blessed me in ways that I never could have imagined. I look back in wonder.

I don't have any desire to try to pick apart all of the answers to prayer, all of the coincidences that faith says were acts of God, and try to rationalize them and reduce them down to being meaningless. More than that, I believe it would likely be impossible for me to do so.

It would take more faith to walk away from faith than to remain in it. I hesitate saying that because I realize many people do not have the same stockpile of significant "God-moments" as I've had. Nevertheless it is true for me.

Even though I've had more than my fair share of those epic moments, they've been fewer in the last decade or so. I love those goose-bump-inducing episodes — especially in corporate gatherings — where it seems God is pressing home his presence. I was never addicted to them, but I am not as reliant on them as I was.

While Jesus rebuked the lukewarm Laodicean church because they'd lost their first love for him, I don't believe that in losing my first faith, I lost my first love. In fact, I'm glad to leave that old skin of faith behind, shed slowly through the years. Back then, I thought the gospel was largely about destination and interim morality—getting people into heaven and hoping that they'd be good in the meantime.

Now, in understanding that the main message of Jesus is the kingdom of God, I realize that we have a message that wonderfully includes eternity, but it is so much bigger than I thought. As we invite people to step into the kingdom under the royal rule of Jesus, we also seek to have organizations, structures, and nations act righteously— the right way—so child slaves who pick cocoa beans for our chocolate are liberated, so injustice is routed, so corporate greed is curtailed. This is the message that profoundly affects absolutely everything: our attitude regarding the environment, politics, social justice, personal morality—the message of Jesus has something to say about every- thing that is human.

I have learned that commitment is not about neurosis and self- flagellation, that guidance is not a code to be cracked or a jigsaw puzzle to be assembled. I have discovered that doubt, far from being something to fear, is a component of faith; trust is impossible with its occasional impingement. Not only that, but as I give myself to the agony of doubt, I am showing how serious I am about believ- ing, ensuring that my faith isn't a flimsy hand-me-down thing, and that it's rugged and resilient enough to stand up to scrutiny. And in turning my back on some of the rickety, untrustworthy slogans of my earlier days, I find a faith that is robust, stronger than I imagined it might be.

I have a thick "pending" file of questions still unanswered, doc- trines that I haven't abandoned but refuse to preach on because those issues remain unclear to me, still in the fog—and I won't feign clar- ity about that which still lies in the mist. But I have learned more deeply that grace can be trusted and that the fundamental summary of the gospel is this: it is good news.

I realize that my faith, though an experience of forty years, has largely been untested by trial. I know very little about suffering. My life has only been tinged with occasional trauma. That still nudges me into anxiety. And so I fear that if, like Peter, I had sat on that beach and heard of what was ahead, I might have given Jesus a warm hug, thanked him for everything—and headed back to the boat and the net.

Who knows?

But for now, with the life I do have, I'm still a joyful, troubled, turbulent, grateful soul, with the unsettled soul of a refugee, a traveler. I am more convinced than ever that Jesus is who he says he is. I have decided.

When it comes to life, he is it.

I am no longer depressed. I have my days when mist gathers, but I'm a little more acquainted with myself than I used to be. When I get low, instead of rebuking dark forces or diving into my hackneyed routines of introspection, I check my sleep patterns, wonder about the jet lag—and then, perhaps, I edge toward those routines of introspection.

I have come to embrace seasons of sadness as a normal, healthy part of the journey. As I write this, my mother is battling the final stages of Alzheimer's disease. Seeing her in such bewilderment and occasional anger is the purest form of torture; I don't need to try to find anything to rejoice about as I helplessly watch her decline.

I embrace the deep sadness that floods my soul when I see her or think about her. I find no purpose in her suffering and don't need to hunt for it. Jesus was and is the model of perfect humanity, and he was extremely familiar with sadness and frustration.

In his book *The Jesus I Never Knew*, Philip Yancey describes how world-renowned author M. Scott Peck was shocked by the Jesus of the gospels:

Scott Peck writes that he first approached the Gospels skepti-cally, suspecting he would find public relations accounts written by authors who had tied together loose ends and embellished their biographies of Jesus. The Gospels themselves quickly dis-abused him of that notion.

He then quotes Peck:

I was absolutely thunderstruck by the extraordinary reality of the man I found in the Gospels. I discovered a man who was almost continuously frustrated. His frustration leaps out of al-most every page. "What do I have to say to you? How many times do I have to say it? What do I have to do to get through to you?" I also discovered a man who was frequently sad and sometimes depressed, frequently anxious and scared ... a man who was terribly, terribly lonely, yet often desperately needed to be alone. I discovered a man so incredibly real that no one could have made Him up....

The Jesus of the Gospels ... did not have much "peace of mind" in the world's terms, and insofar as we can be his follow-ers, perhaps we won't either.

The preacher in me feels the need to explain in alliterated detail why it is that I remain absolutely determined to continue to be an apprentice of Christ. But this much I know: somehow, in my gut, in the core of who I am, he has changed me. I never was a fisherman, but if I had been, the nets wouldn't work for me anymore. And even though I don't fully know why, the song the congregation sang on the night of my baptism remains true.

I have decided to follow Jesus, no turning back.

No turning back.

10

...

MIND YOUR OWN BUSINESS

Peter turned and saw that the disciple whom Jesus loved was following them. (This was the one who had leaned back against Jesus at the supper and had said, "Lord, who is going to betray you?") When Peter saw him, he asked, "Lord, what about him?" Jesus answered, "If I want him to remain alive until I return, what is that to you? You must follow me." Because of this, the rumor spread among the believers that this disciple would not die. But Jesus did not say that he would not die; he only said, "If I want him to remain alive until I return, what is that to you?"

JOHN 21:20–23

You ascended from before our eyes, and we turned back grieving, only to find you in our hearts.

AUGUSTINE

All your dissatisfaction with the Church seems to me to come from an incomplete understanding of sin.... the Church is founded on Peter who denied Christ three times and couldn't walk on water by himself. You are expecting his successors to walk on water. All human nature vigorously resists grace because grace changes us and the change is painful. Priests resist it as well as others. To have the Church be what you want it to be would require the miraculous meddling of God in human affairs.

FLANNERY O'CONNOR

have wondered how I would react if the doctor, bland face fixed in professional deadpan, gave me the verdict: It's very serious, Mr. Lucas. I'm afraid there's absolutely nothing we can do. I'm very sorry. Get your affairs in order.

What would I do?

I'd love to believe that I'd take the brutal punch of the diagnosis with a set jaw, eyes shining, resolute and brave. I'd like to think that I'd say something heroic about how living is Christ and dying is gain, that I'd thank the doctor for his forthrightness, who would in turn stammer out that he was amazed at my faith, and that maybe he should become a Christian too, and could we pray now? But I fear that I'd collapse in a blubbering heap and emerge from the clinic with reddened, blotchy eyes. Those in the waiting room would stare at me, knowingly.

Aha. He's the source of that wailing we heard a few moments ago.

Brave or wretched, lionhearted or coward, one thing's for certain: If a death sentence was handed down to me, I'd hand a few questions back.

Lots of them.

But Peter had no opportunity to ask all those questions, to have the blanks filled in, because his moment of privacy with Jesus was interrupted.

It was John, suddenly showing up, interrupting one of the most critical moments of Peter's life, without so much as an invitation.

John.

The disciple whom Jesus loved.

Peter is desperately trying to process the staggering news, to allow it to sink in, but before he gets a chance to get any further clarity, John shows up, immediately shattering this deeply intimate, private moment.

And so Peter, having been told his most difficult destiny, points over at John and asks, "What about him?" More than an academic question, perhaps it was a question borne of insecurity. Once again we're reminded not just that John showed up, but that it was John, the disciple whom Jesus loved. Is there a clue in that statement that helps us to understand Peter's question?

Here's what I imagine might have been in Peter's head:

I've just told you that I love you, Jesus. Three times, no less. And your response? A commission, yes, to feed the sheep, but then you give me this news of my death. I love you, and what do I get? Martyrdom. So now what about this John, this confidante of yours, this friend that you shared your closest secrets with? What kind of future does he get, Jesus? Does he get the death sentence too? Or is he spared that because you love him too much to allow him to go through that? And if that's the case, what does that say about how you feel about me?

Or perhaps, just perhaps, Peter was not just troubled by John's intrusion, but was bristling at the injustice of it all. We often struggle when we feel that not only are we being dealt a bad hand—the other guy is getting a royal flush.

"It's not fair" is one of the phrases we learn early in life. We feel it when we don't have the toy that the kid next door has, when it rains on our day out at the seaside, or when that big guy in school bullies us. It's not fair. We'd like pain to be distributed evenly, for when someone gets the better deal, the unearned promotion, we smart.

Perhaps we'd do well to settle this rather unwelcome truth now: life isn't fair. Peter will be martyred, and John, although he walked through his own seasons of pain and exile, would die of old age. There's no even distribution of suffering, and Jesus doesn't promise that there would be.

Or perhaps there's another reason for Peter's question: maybe he didn't want to go into his valley of pain alone and would have found the news that John would also suffer—perhaps with him—of great comfort.

Or maybe he just wanted to know what was really none of his business.

If you've been part of a church for more than six months and nobody in it or nothing about it has irritated you yet, then you're probably clinically dead. But some people spend a lot of their lives pondering the question, What about him? or What about that? as I recently discovered, to my dismay.

• • •

One of the ministers at our church irritates me. He's probably a nice enough chap, but I'm finding his preaching rather boring, and he preaches a lot. Sometimes I groan when I know it's him again. I'm sure he works hard at sermon preparation, and he probably sincerely wants to impact people for God. He tries hard, peppering his talks with anecdotes and warm humor. But recently I reached the point where I decided that if I had to listen to him preach just one more time, I'd end up breaking something.

The trouble is, there's absolutely nothing I can do about it, because that preacher is me. One of the drawbacks of a busy speaking ministry is that I listen to myself a lot. When I'm home in Colorado, I hear myself preach the same message four times over in a weekend: the same outline, the same points, even the same "spontaneous" humor. It's gets old, hearing me.

Recently I shared my frustration with my ever-patient wife, Kay. "I preach so much, I get sick of the sound of my own voice," I muttered.

She proffered a smile of quiet resignation. "Yes darling," she said. "I understand completely how you feel."

So it came as welcome relief to go to a church and hear somebody else preach for a change. We decided to visit a local church from a denomination quite different from our own. Soft rock worship is replaced by the throaty tones of an ancient pipe organ. The smell of incense hangs heavy in the air, which presents me with the challenge of coughing reverently. And the minister has that singsong parsonical voice. When it comes to style, it's Mars to our Venus.

But as we made our way in through the ancient porch, I whispered a note to myself: I love diversity. Years of involvement in events like Spring Harvest, a long-established conference of teaching and worship attended by many thousands, have taught me that my way is not the high way, that I have so much to learn from Christians who express their faith in other styles. Our differences are to be celebrated and respected, I've learned. Or so I thought.

Slipping into an unyielding wooden pew that morning, waiting for the service to begin, I suddenly realized that I was irritated with myself again—and I wasn't even preaching. To my horror, I discovered that I was already anticipating that I would bristle at what was about to happen. I'd surely tut-tut at the slightly out-of-tune organ, I'd be frustrated with that clerical voice, and I'd definitely be bored by the sermon, which I'd already decided would be desperately dull. I was warming up to be offended before the proceedings had even begun.

What was wrong with me?

The service began with a kind welcome, the singing got underway, and then it was time for the sermon. I settled back and got ready to be frustrated by the tedium to come, but to my amazement, the talk was brilliant. Accessible, biblical, and engaging, the minister spoke with clarity and confidence. It was outstanding.

But here's the part I'd rather keep to myself: as the final hymn concluded, the organ pitch-perfect, I realized that I was actually disappointed to not be disappointed. How sick is that? I'd gone to church anticipating that I wouldn't like it, and then felt deflated because my prejudices had not been confirmed. I was offended because I had no reason to be offended. The service over, we filed out. I shook the minister's hand and thanked him for such a wonderful sermon.

There's a certain myopia that comes with a critical heart. We decide that we don't like somebody, or come to a quiet, negative conclusion about the church we attend, and then the filtering begins. When we see a fault, we zoom in on it, triumphantly holding it up as Exhibit A, evidence that proves we're in the right, which is where we like to be. Or, like me, we book our tickets for a seat in the offended section well in advance. But then we ignore or minimize the good things that that person or church does, or even bristle when someone we've tagged as suspect actually does something well.

Yikes. We can't have that, for it shows we might actually be wrong.

So I'm back to being irritated with that minister at our church again, the one called me. This time, it's not just because I get to hear my voice a lot; it's because I don't want a pompous, judgmental heart. This much is certain: if I hear myself preach a sermon on being negative and critical anytime soon, I'll be the first in line to respond.

• • •

Often when people yell, "What about him?" they drop the h-bomb: *Hypocrite*.

It's a term I've often heard from those who have drifted or marched away from church; I hoped for so much. We were going to change the world together. But then I realized the truth. They're all just a bunch of hypocrites.

The word is often used unfairly. A hypocrite is not someone whose life does not completely match their beliefs—if that's the cold definition, then we're all hypocrites, because we all are incomplete travelers on the journey.

A hypocrite is someone who deliberately playacts, who puts on a pious mask and pretends to have arrived. Granted, there are a few of

those about too, but when we throw the h-bomb around indiscrimi-
nately, we judge harshly.

But whether we're asking, "What about that person?" because
we're irritated with another flawed follower of Jesus, or whether we're
frustrated because of blatant pretenders deserving of Oscars for their
performances, we should never gamble our confidence on the fragile
consistency of others—or ourselves, for that matter.

Sometimes an obsession with the question "What about ...?" is
sparked by the small irritations of church life:

That "godly" gossiper.

The know-it-all who unwittingly has succumbed to spiritual
pride.

Those intercessors who berate everyone else because they don't
want to pray at 4:00 a.m.

Or that sentry at the entry gate of the beach who insisted that I
yank down my shorts, covering a little more of my legs, but exposing
the top of my very untanned rear end to the world.

I approached the exit to that beach with a little trepidation, and
even though I was on my way out (so he couldn't exclude me), he
could still send me away with a parting shot of disapproval. I had
enjoyed my time at the beach, even if I'd initially felt so clumsily out
of place, and I didn't want it spoiled by a scowling priest.

I sped up my walk, hoping to steer past him briskly, avoid any
conversation, and not catch his eye. As it was, he was busy giving
some other sufficiently "immodest" person a hard time.

It was then that I noticed something about him that made me
want to laugh and cry.

He too was wearing shorts.

• • •

I love the way Jesus talks straight to Peter—and I'm also mildly terrified of it. Instead of tiptoeing around issues, Jesus often gets right

to the point. Instead of gently edging Peter away from the distracting subject of what would happen to John, Jesus effectively says, "Mind your own business." Jesus wouldn't tell Peter John's story, but only his own. Peter was left in absolutely no doubt — to pursue this line of questioning about John's future would not be a good idea.

Perhaps this is not just straight talking, but tender, caring talk as well. It must have hurt Jesus to tell Peter about what lay ahead, especially as Jesus knew very well what it felt like to be condemned and executed.

I don't believe that Jesus delivered that prophetic news with cold, harsh indifference; on the contrary, perhaps Jesus knew that Peter had more than enough to deal with as he grappled with the news that pain and death lay ahead. Perhaps Jesus didn't want him to clutter his mind and complicate things further by wrestling with questions that ultimately didn't concern him. He just needed to focus on responding to the further invitation, now solemnly given: Follow me.

What would his response be?

• • •

It is roughly six weeks later, and Peter has no idea about the significance of the day that has dawned so ordinarily, like any other day. It's a birthday — the church's birthday — but he doesn't know that yet, as Jerusalem teems with pilgrims, gathered for the Pentecost celebrations.

Peter couldn't know that he was about to preach one of the shortest but most effective sermons in history, or that stupendous miracles are just around the corner. He was to be the kingdom spokesperson as he delivered his first sermon on the day of Pentecost.

He was stronger after their epic experience, when 120 of them had gathered in an upper room. Suddenly, they'd heard a strange, unearthly sound, and then fire flickered. Mysteriously, they were speaking in languages they'd never learned. Jesus didn't walk in on them again. He had gone away—gone up—just like he'd said. But somehow, when the wind blew, it felt like it was him in a way that they couldn't explain. More than power, this power had personality. The Spirit of Christ. The Holy Spirit.

There was nothing discreet or contained about this experience they'd had. The noise of it summoned a crowd, some intrigued, others mocking. The air was thick with jeers about them, being nothing more than a bunch of drunks, a gang of ignorant fishermen from the Galilee and their friends, boisterous in their celebrations, too long at the wine. That's them. The gawping, giggling crowd was waiting, demanding to know.

What does all this mean?

It was time.

It was Peter's moment and the disciples' moment together. Quickly, he looked around at the others, and their eyes, their nods silently confirmed what he already knew was true: they were with him.

Bring it on.

All was ready.

Slowly, deliberately, he rose to his feet.

ACKNOWLEDGMENTS

My appreciation and gratitude to the team at Zondervan, who collectively exhibited the fruit of the Spirit — especially patience — while waiting for the manuscript of this book. Special thanks to Sue Brower, the editor who, through no fault of her own, was around for the conception of this book, but not its birth. To Londa Alderink, for cover concepts, marketing, and general all-round kindness, and to John Sloan, an editor whose head, helpfully, does not revolve 360 degrees, but whose brain does. To Bob Hudson, not only for his skills as "Editor-in-Chief," but for words of warm encouragement.

Thanks to Dr. Donald McCullough, a man I have never met but have briefly corresponded with. His writing moves, inspires, and intimidates me in turn. His book *The Wisdom of Pelicans* is the beautiful work of a supremely gifted wordsmith and, more importantly, an incredibly brave soul. Someone has said that writers are called to sit down, pen in hand, and open a vein. Your candor has spurred me to be candid, Dr. McCullough, and I'm most grateful. In this book, I quote him frequently and without apology: *Pelicans* is the book of the decade for me.

My love and thanks to the wonderfully welcoming church family at the Elim Church, Barking, London, who ushered me from the cold. Special appreciation to Pastor Brian Richardson, whose infectious smile, inspiring preaching, and pastoral kindness helped nurse me through the early years, and to Pam Richardson, now with Jesus, whose smile and care first made me think of Him.

Gratitude also to David and Valerie Norman, extraordinary youth leaders; and to Malcolm Thompson, who crossed the room that night and asked me the biggest question of my life.

Finally, thanks to my dear friends Ishmael and Irene Smale, who battled through the deep fog that billows out of nowhere when leukemia strikes and then knew they would have to be brave in the face of the loss of their beloved grandson Quinn. Your example shows me that I know something about having faith in the fog, but not a lot.

Jeff Lucas
Colorado, 2013

NOTES

15: *Why does the sea attract me:* E. B. White, *The Sea and the Wind that Blows: Essays of E. B. White* (New York: Harper, 1977), 206.

15: *Every time we walk along a beach:* Loren Eiseley, *The Unexpected Universe* (San Diego: Harcourt, 1977), 51.

15: *The sea does not reward those who are too anxious:* Anne Morrow Lindbergh, *Gift from the Sea* (New York: Vintage, 1955), 16–17.

16: *like a watery earthquake:* Matthew 8:24. The original Greek suggests "an earthquake at sea," but only the Aramaic Bible in Plain English brings "earthquake" into its translation. All the other major Bibles simply refer to it as a violent storm or tempest.

18: *now it's down to 20 percent:* online.wsj.com/article/SB10001424052748704 304504574610022765965390.html.

31: *Nostalgia is the suffering:* Milan Kundera, *Ignorance*, trans. Linda Asher (New York: HarperCollins, 2002), 5.

32–33: *I've never thought of myself as someone who clings to the past:* Monica A. Coleman, *Not Alone: Reflections on Faith and Depression* (Culver City, Calif.: Inner Prizes, 2012), 168.

33: *they would meet Jesus in Galilee:* Matthew 28:7; Mark 16:7.

33: *the worshiping women on Easter morning:* Matthew 28:10.

34: *The little band of friends and followers:* Luke 24:38.

35: *They thought they'd seen a ghost:* Luke 24:37.

35: *Joy mingled with their amazement:* Luke 24:41.

35: *They needed to have their minds "opened" to understand:* Luke 24:35.

35: *They were afraid yet filled with joy:* Matthew 28:8.

35: *They worshiped, but some doubted:* Matthew 28:17.

35: *They were trembling, bewildered, and afraid:* Mark 16:8.

35: *They stubbornly refused to believe:* Mark 16:14.

35: *They gathered fearfully behind locked doors:* John 20:19.

35: *They were overjoyed:* John 20:20.

35: *There is neither the joy nor the assurance:* D. A. Carson, *The Gospel According to John* (Grand Rapids: Eerdmans, 1990), 670.

36: *forty-day training period:* Acts 1:3.

36: *he'd tried to prepare them for the parting:* John 14:26.

36: *vandalized a roof, hacking through it:* Mark 2:4.

37: *turning it into a makeshift pulpit:* Luke 5:1–3.

37: *five thousand fed to the full:* Matthew 14:13–21.

37: *Now they were welcomed in from the cold:* Luke 17:11–19.

37: *gale-force winds had calmed at his word:* Mark 4:35–41.

37: *Will you leave also?:* John 6:67.

38: *He was arrested, and everyone fled:* Mark 14:50.

38: *They'd planned to take him home forcibly:* Matthew 12:46–50.

38: *who was the greatest among them?:* Luke 9:46.

38: *It's mentioned twice in Scripture:* Luke 24:34; 1 Cor. 15:5.

39: *he briefly strode across the waves:* Matthew 14:22–33.

40: *introduced by his brother Andrew:* John 1:41–42.

40: *he had a wife:* 1 Corinthians 9:5.

40: *she'd recovered at a touch from Jesus:* Matthew 8:14ff.

41: *the girl's stunned parents witnessed her being raised:* Mark 5:35–43.

41: *who Jesus really was and is:* Matthew 17:1–7.

41: *a little huddle in Gethsemane:* Matthew 26:36–46.

42: *How many times is enough?:* Matthew 18:21.

42: *Don't you know everyone's looking for you?:* Mark 1:35–39.

42: *he didn't bother to go to the house:* Luke 7:1–10.

42: *He'd put his fingers into people's ears:* Mark 7:33.

42: *spit mixed with mud onto blind eyes:* John 9:6.

42: *then apparently run from it:* Matthew 8:18.

42: *a hand of blessing upon their children:* Matthew 19:13.

43: *but merely human concerns:* Matthew 16:23.

44: *Jesus called a halt to the fight and healed the man:* John 18:10; Luke 22:51.

44: *the rooster crowed for the third time:* Luke 22:61.

46: *My Lord and my God:* John 20:28.

46: *Nathaniel had declared that Jesus was the Son of God:* John 1:45–51.

47: *Illusions commend themselves to us:* Sigmund Freud, *Reflections on War and Death* (New York: Moffat, Yard and Co., 1918), 16.

47: *I started writing about my own experiences:* Monica A. Coleman, *Not Alone: Reflections on Faith and Depression* (Culver City, Calif.: Inner Prizes, 2012), xi.

47: *Now faith, in the sense in which I am here using the word:* C. S. Lewis, *Mere Christianity* (San Francisco: HarperOne, 2012; orig. 1952), 186.

47: *About midnight the fog shut down:* Captain Joshua Slocum, *Sailing Alone around the World* (New York: Century, 1900), 26.

59: *Therefore, if anyone is in Christ:* 2 Corinthians 5:17.

62: *When wisdom entereth into thine heart:* Proverbs 2:10, 16–19 KJV.

64–65: *even though the scriptural passage they cited:* Colossians 3:15.

73: *Somehow, in the midst of our tears:* Henri J. M. Nouwen, *With Burning Hearts* (Maryknoll, N.Y.: Orbis, 2003), 28.

73: *We are here to abet creation:* Annie Dillard quoted in David Friend, ed., *The Meaning of Life* (Boston: Little Brown, 1991).

75: *Nicodemus used the cover of night:* John 3:2.

75: *Judas deserted Jesus under the same canopy:* John 13:30.

75: *Resurrection morning was shrouded in darkness:* John 20:1.

75: *at nighttime the disciples huddled:* John 20:19.

76: *You give them something to eat:* Mark 6:37.

76: *the lack of faith of his hapless apprentices:* Matthew 17:17.

77: *How long, LORD, must I call for help:* Habakkuk 1:2.

77–78: *My God, my God, why have you forsaken me?:* Psalm 22: 1, 2, 19.

78: *My God, my God, why have you forsaken me?:* Matthew 27:46

78: *we are never abandoned by God:* 2 Corinthians 4:9.

78: *Never will I leave you:* Hebrews 13:5.

79: *And speaking of God, where is he?:* Donald McCullough, *The Wisdom of Pelicans: A Search for Healing at the Water's Edge* (New York: Penguin, 2002), 7.

79: *A question troubles me:* McCullough, *Wisdom of Pelicans*, 38.

80: *The next two years were marked by a slow descent:* Peter Scazzero with Warren Bird, *The Emotionally Healthy Church* (Grand Rapids: Zondervan, 2002), 29.

80: *He was a bent old man:* Elie Wiesel, *Night* (New York: Bantam, 1960), 72–73.

81: *Jesus has a very special love for you:* Quoted in David Van Biema, "Mother Teresa's Crisis of Faith," *Time* magazine (Thursday, Aug. 23, 2007).

81: *Darkness is such that I really do not see:* Mother Teresa, *Come Be My Light: The Revealing Private Writings of the Nobel Peace Prize Winner* (New York: Doubleday, 2007), 211.

81: *I've never read a saint's life:* Read more: http://www.time.com/time /magazine/article/0,9171,1655720,00.html#ixzz2AhG7aECN.

82: *What we need is a radical sense of exile:* Alan Jones, *The Soul's Journey* (San Francisco: HarperSanFrancisco, 1995), 47.

83: *they were kept from recognizing him:* Luke 24:16.

83: *when the risen Jesus met the weeping Mary:* John 20:15.

84: *James and John requested thrones:* Matthew 20:17ff.

84: *they thought he was going to restore the kingdom:* Acts 1:6.

84: *He's pledged his presence, forever and always:* Matthew 28:20.

85: *For now we see only a reflection as in a mirror:* 1 Corinthians 13:12.

86: *psalms, hymns, and songs from the Spirit:* Ephesians 5:19.

87: *To whom shall we go?:* John 6:68.

88: *We have locked God into the so-called sacred realms:* Michael Frost, *Seeing God in the Ordinary: A Theology of the Everyday* (Grand Rapids: Baker, 2000), 33, 16.

89: *Our churches are filled with people:* Keith Miller, *The Taste of New Wine* (Waco, Tx.: Word, 1965), 22.

93: *I am writing to you, dear children:* 1 John 2:12.

93: *Dear children, this is the last hour:* 1 John 2:18.

93: *his yoke being easy, and his burden light:* Matthew 11:30.

93–94: *People were bringing little children to Jesus:* Mark 10:13–16.

95: *How unutterably sweet is the knowledge:* A. W. Tozer, *The Knowledge of the Holy* (New York: Harper & Row, 1961), 63.

96–97: *Once when he was standing on the shore of Lake Gennesaret:* Luke 5:1–11, Eugene Peterson, *The Message: The Bible in Contemporary Language* (Colorado Springs: NavPress, 2005).

99: *This was not a rationed snack:* Matthew 14:13–21.

99: *120 gallons of wonderful wine:* John 2:1–11.

99–100: *And I ask him that with both feet planted firmly:* Ephesians 3:17–20, Peterson, *Message.*

100: *it's John who sees and understands:* John 20:4–8.

101–102: *For no matter how significant you are:* 1 Corinthians 12:19–27, Peterson, *Message.*

102–3: *Then Jesus went with them to a garden:* Matthew 26:36–46, Peterson, *Message.*

103: *sociologist Robert Putnam suggests:* Robert D. Putnam, *Bowling Alone: The Collapse and Revival of American Culture* (New York: Simon & Schuster, 2000).

104: *I can do all things through Christ:* Philippians 4:13 NKJV.

105: *This team, which had once been threatened by pettiness:* Luke 9:46.

105: *Jesus had taught them to act like servants:* Mark 10:42–45.

107: *Christianity, from Golgotha onwards:* Malcolm Muggeridge quoted in R. Kent Hughes, *John: That You May Believe* (Wheaton, Ill.: Crossway, 1999), 464.

107: *He saw with eyes that saw everything:* John Tambourine, *The Other Nietzsche,* ebook (books.google.co.uk), 50.

109: *It was cold, and the servants and officials stood around a fire:* John 18:18.

109: *Meanwhile, Simon Peter was still standing there warming himself:* John 18:25.

111: *I had placed myself behind my own back:* Augustine, *Confessions,* Pine-Coffin, trans. (London: Penguin, 1985), 169.

111: *My preferred method of dealing with ugliness:* McCullough, *Wisdom of Pelicans,* 20.

112–13: *We read, we hear, we believe a good theology of grace:* David A. Seamands, *Healing for Damaged Emotions Workbook* (Colorado Springs: David C. Cook, 2001), 43.

113–14: *Jesus knew that the Father had put all things under his power:* John 13:3–9.

115: *I will not let you go unless you bless me:* Genesis 32:26 NLT.

116: *My people would not listen to me:* Psalm 81:11 NLT.

116: *I think that if God forgives us we must forgive ourselves:* C. S. Lewis, in a letter to Miss Breckenridge, *The Collected Letters of C. S. Lewis, Volume III* (New York: HarperCollins, 2007), 109.

118: *My life has been spent in vain and idle aspirations:* Quoted in John Ortberg, *The Life You've Always Wanted: Spiritual Disciplines for Ordinary People* (Grand Rapids: Zondervan, 2002), 163.

119: *To make conscience into God:* J. B. Phillips, *Your God Is Too Small: A Guide for Believers and Skeptics Alike* (New York: Touchstone, 1952), 15.

120–21: *John—not his real name—was a bright, popular guy:* Jeff Lucas, *Grace Choices* (Milton Keynes, UK: Authentic Lifestyle, 2005), 75–76.

124: *All the people saw this and began to mutter:* Luke 19:7.

124: *Now the tax collectors and sinners were all gathering:* Luke 15:1–2.

124: *He touched untouchables with love:* Colin Buchanan, ed., *Anglican Eucharistic Liturgies, 1985–2010,* "Eucharistic Prayer D" (London: Canterbury, 2010), 41.

124: *He saw heaven opened:* Acts 10:11–16.

127: *Your brain is physically injured:* Jerod Poore, blog posting quoted at crazymeds.us/CrazyTalk/index.php?/topic/1795-medications-as-band-aids/

131: *moved into the neighborhood:* John 1:14, Peterson, *Message.*

132: *For we do not have a high priest:* Hebrews 4:15–16.

134: *In the United States, 5 to 10 percent:* Daniel G. Blazer, "The Depression Epidemic" (christianitytoday.com/ct/2009/march/15.22.html). Dr. Daniel G. Blazer is J. P. Gibbons Professor of Psychiatry and Behavioral Sciences at Duke University Medical Center and author of *The Age of Melancholy: Major Depression and Its Social Origins* (New York: Routledge, 2005).

134–35: *After weeks of therapy:* Mark Mounts, "It Can't Be Depression, I'm a Christian" (gci.org/CO/depression).

136: *With prayer, "all things are possible":* Mark Mounts, "It Can't Be Depression, I'm a Christian" (gci.org/CO/depression).

136: *broken bodies and brains that need fixing:* Blazer, "The Depression Epidemic."

137–38: *The "normal" human life isn't what is marketed to us:* Russell D. Moore, "Is It Right for a Christian to Take Anti-Depressants?" (russellmoore.com /2012/02/28/is-it-right-for-a-christian-to-take-anti-depressants/).

138–39: *There are some Christians who believe:* Moore, "Is It Right for a Christian to Take Anti-Depressants?"

139: *Just then his disciples returned:* John 4:27.

140–41: *The disciples had been granted:* Carson, *Gospel According to John*, 674.

141: *Looking toward the horizon:* McCullough, *Wisdom of Pelicans*, 8.

143: *One result of the mysterious nature of love:* Scott Peck, *The Road Less Traveled* (New York: Touchstone, 1978), 81.

147: *Blessed are you, Simon son of Jonah:* Matthew 16:17–18.

148: *Come, follow me, … and I will send you out to fish for people:* Matthew 4:19.

149: *Hearing that Jesus had silenced the Sadducees:* Matthew 22:34–40.

149: *Anyone who loves their father or mother:* Matthew 10:37.

150: *It's wrong, and I try not to sing wrong lyrics:* johnstackhouse.com/2007/09 /16/jesus-im-not-in-love-with-you/.

151: *When a person falls in love:* Peck, *Road Less Traveled*, 84.

153: *Love is an action, an activity:* Peck, *Road Less Traveled*, 116.

155–56: *You are accepted:* Paul Tillich, *The Shaking of the Foundations* (New York: Scribner, 1948), 162.

156: *If you love me, keep my commands:* John 14:15.

157: *You ask me what forgiveness means:* Rita F. Snowden, *I Believe in the Dawn* (London: Epworth, 1958).

158: *This is how we know that we belong:* 1 John 3:19–20.

159: *It must be realized that the true sign:* Quoted in Igumen Chariton, *The Art of Prayer: An Orthodox Anthology* (New York: Macmillan, 1997), 117. Russian monk and, later, bishop, Theophan the Recluse (1815–94) is a saint in the Russian Orthodox Church.

159: *All the great religions were first preached:* C. S. Lewis, *The Problem of Pain* (New York: Macmillan, 1973), 4.

161: *Days earlier, Peter had pledged:* Luke 22:33.

161: *He'd told them clearly about his trial:* Matthew 20:18.

161: *He'd specially told Peter:* Luke 22:31.

161: *He'd even predicted the number of times:* Luke 22:34.

162–63: *O Lord, remember not only the men and women:* bible.org/illustration /concentration-camp-letter.

164: *the promise of Jesus that life in this world:* John 16:33.

165: *Undeniably, in the ministry of Jesus:* Matthew 13:58.

166: *to pray your kingdom come, your will be done:* Matthew 6:10.

167: *For a little while you may have had to suffer:* 1 Peter 1:6–7.

167: *If you are insulted because of the name of Christ:* 1 Peter 4:14–16.

168: *To the elders among you, I appeal:* 1 Peter 5:1.

171: *The fourth step of humility is accepting:* Saint Benedict quoted in Richard J. Foster and James Bryan Smith, *Devotional Classics* (San Francisco:

HarperOne, 2005), 179. Benedict (480–547) founded monasteries in the sixth century and wrote the famous *Rule of Saint Benedict.*

171: *Does the road wind up-hill all the way?* Christina Rossetti, "Up-hill," *The Complete Poems* (London and New York: Penguin, 2001), 59–60.

171: *I cannot read. I cannot think:* Hudson Taylor quoted in Pete Grieg, *God on Mute: Engaging the Silence of Unanswered Prayer* (Ventura, Calif.: Regal, 2007), 6.

173: *On hearing it, many of his disciples said:* John 6:60–69.

174: *Let us also go, that we may die:* John 11:16.

182–83: *Scott Peck writes that he first approached:* Philip Yancey, *The Jesus I Never Knew* (Grand Rapids: Zondervan, 1995), 257.

183: *I was absolutely thunderstruck:* M. Scott Peck, *Further Along the Road Less Traveled* (New York: Simon and Schuster, 1993), 160.

185: *You ascended from before our eyes:* Saint Augustine quoted in Yancey, *The Jesus I Never Knew*, 228.

185: *All your dissatisfaction with the Church:* Flannery O'Connor, *The Habit of Being* (New York: Vintage, 1979), 307.

FOR FURTHER READING

Chariton, Igumen. *The Art of Prayer: An Orthodox Anthology*. New York: Macmillan, 1997.

Coleman, Monica A. *Not Alone: Reflections on Faith and Depression—A 40-Day Devotional*. Culver City, Calif.: Inner Prizes, 2012.

Foster, Richard J., and James Bryan Smith. *Devotional Classics*. San Francisco: HarperOne, 2005.

Frost, Michael. *Seeing God in the Ordinary: A Theology of the Everyday*. Grand Rapids: Baker, 2000.

Grieg, Pete. *God on Mute: Engaging the Silence of Unanswered Prayer*. Ventura, Calif.: Regal, 2007.

Jones, Alan. *The Soul's Journey*. San Francisco: HarperSanFrancisco, 1995.

Lewis, C. S. *Mere Christianity*. San Francisco: HarperOne, 2012; orig. 1952.

McCullough, Donald. *The Wisdom of Pelicans: A Search for Healing at the Water's Edge*. New York: Penguin, 2002.

Nouwen, Henri J. M. *With Burning Hearts*. Maryknoll, N.Y.: Orbis, 2003.

O'Connor, Flannery. *The Habit of Being*. New York: Vintage, 1979.

Ortberg, John. *The Life You've Always Wanted: Spiritual Disciplines for Ordinary People*. Grand Rapids: Zondervan, 2002.

Peck, M. Scott. *Further Along the Road Less Traveled*. New York: Simon and Schuster, 1993.

————. *The Road Less Traveled*. New York: Touchstone, 1978.

Phillips, J. B. *Your God Is Too Small: A Guide for Believers and Skeptics Alike*. New York: Touchstone, 1952.

Putnam, Robert D. *Bowling Alone: The Collapse and Revival of American Culture*. New York: Simon & Schuster, 2000.

Scazzero, Peter, with Warren Bird. *The Emotionally Healthy Church*. Grand Rapids: Zondervan, 2002.

Seamands, David A. *Healing for Damaged Emotions Workbook*. Colorado Springs: David C. Cook, 2001.

Snowden, Rita F. *I Believe in the Dawn*. London: Epworth, 1958.

Snyder, Howard. *The Problem of Wineskins*. Downers Grove, Ill.: InterVarsity, 1975.

Teresa, Mother. *Come Be My Light: The Revealing Private Writings of the Nobel Peace Prize Winner*. New York: Doubleday, 2007.

Tozer, A. W. *The Knowledge of the Holy*. New York: Harper & Row, 1961.

Wiesel, Elie. *Night*. New York: Bantam, 1960.

Yancey, Philip. *The Jesus I Never Knew*. Grand Rapids: Zondervan, 1995.

Heaven Help Helen Sloane

A Novel

J. R. Lucas

Helen Sloane is in for one interesting year.
Written as a series of journal entries, *Heaven
Help Helen Sloane* is refreshingly honest,
poignant, and often hilarious, documenting—
in Helen's own words—the daily struggles a
young Christian woman must face. Helen's new job as a social worker
keeps her busy all day in a whirlwind of case notes and court papers,
and at home she's a house group leader for Frenton-on-Sea's New
Wave Christian Fellowship. She loves her church, but she struggles
with faith and doubt, exposed to the religious extremes of both
hyperspiritual friends and her New Age mom. And with her busy
schedule, Helen also struggles to make time for love. Still, she finds
two men in her life: a handsome worship leader who might not be
as godly as he seems, and a former Christian turned Bohemian bad
boy. Can she keep her faith strong in the midst of a chaotic life? Jeff
Lucas answers this question through the joy, tragedy, love, and heart-
break revealed in the pages of Helen Sloane's journal.

Available in stores and online!

ZONDERVAN®
.com

Share Your Thoughts

With the Author: Your comments will be forwarded to the author when you send them to *zauthor@zondervan.com*.

With Zondervan: Submit your review of this book by writing to *zreview@zondervan.com*.

Free Online Resources at

www.zondervan.com

Daily Bible Verses and Devotions: Enrich your life with daily Bible verses or devotions that help you start every morning focused on God. Visit www.zondervan.com/newsletters.

Free Email Publications: Sign up for newsletters on Christian living, academic resources, church ministry, fiction, children's resources, and more. Visit www.zondervan.com/newsletters.

Zondervan Bible Search: Find and compare Bible passages in a variety of translations at www.zondervanbiblesearch.com.

Other Benefits: Register to receive online benefits like coupons and special offers, or to participate in research.